PACIFIC
ISLANDS

MITHS AND WONDERS OF THE SOUTHERN SEAS

WHITE STAR
PUBLISHERS

Texts
Marco Moretti

Graphic design
Anna Galliani

Translation
Neil Frazer Davenport

PACIFIC ISLANDS
MITHS AND WONDERS OF THE SOUTHERN SEAS

CONTENTS

1 One of the atolls of the Tuamotu group, an archipelago in French Polynesia situated north-east of Tahiti and composed of 78 rings of land enclosing lagoons and numerous coral reefs scattered across some hundreds of thousands of square miles of ocean.

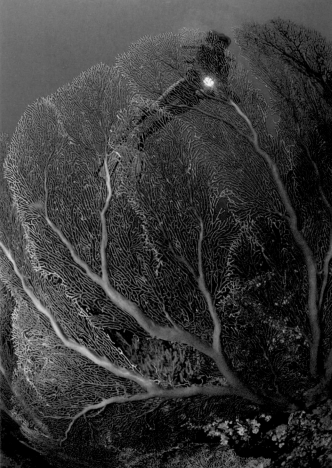

©1999, 2004 White Star S.r.l.,
Via Candido Sassone 22/24,
13100 Vercelli, Italy.
www.whitestar.it

ISBN 88-544-0011-4
Reprints:
1 2 3 4 5 6   08 07 06 05 04

Color separations Fotomec Turin
Printed in China by C & C Offset
Printing Co.

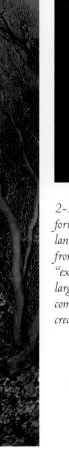

2-3 Rangiroa's Blue Lagoon is formed within the narrow strip of land dividing the internal lagoon from the open ocean. Rangiroa means "extension of the sky" and is the largest of the Polynesian atolls. It is composed of 249 motus which create a ring of and 143 miles long.

4-5 Whitehaven Beach is the most spectacular in the Whitsundays, the largest archipelago of the coast of Queensland (north-western Australia). The 74 rocky islands cloaked in tropical vegetation are Australia's principal sailing destination.

6 top One of the moais of Easter Island where the most far-flung society resulting from the Polynesian diaspora sculpted 886 statues with human features from volcanic tufa. These monoliths are between 6.5 and 72 feet tall (the Great Moai) and are scattered across the barren hills.

6 bottom This photo shows a variety of coral from New Caledonia, the Melanesian archipelago (French overseas territory) boasting the world's second largest barrier reef which is over 990 miles long and encloses a lagoon of 8,900 square miles.

6-7 Lord Howe Island, located 435 miles from Australia (to which it belongs), is halfway between New Zealand and New Caledonia and divides the cold waters of the Tasman Sea from the warm Coral Sea. In spite of its Polynesian appearance it has a temperate climate.

ASIA

MARIANA ISLANDS

PALAU ISLANDS

M I C R O N E S I A

MARSHALL ISLANDS

CAROLINE ISLANDS

M E L A N E S I A

• Jayapura

New Guinea

• Port Moresby

SOLOMON ISLANDS

SAMOA

VANUATU

FIJI

Darwin •

Cape York Peninsula

• Noumea

New Caledonia

TONGA

INDIAN
OCEAN

NORTHERN
TERRITORY

QUEENSLAND

WESTERN
AUSTRALIA

AUSTRALIA

SOUTH
AUSTRALIA

Brisbane •

NEW SOUTH
WALES

• Sydney

Auckland •

NORTH ISLAND

Perth •

Adelaide •

VICTORIA

New Zeland

• Wellington

• Melbourne

Christchurch •

• Hobart

TASMANIA

SOUTH ISLAND

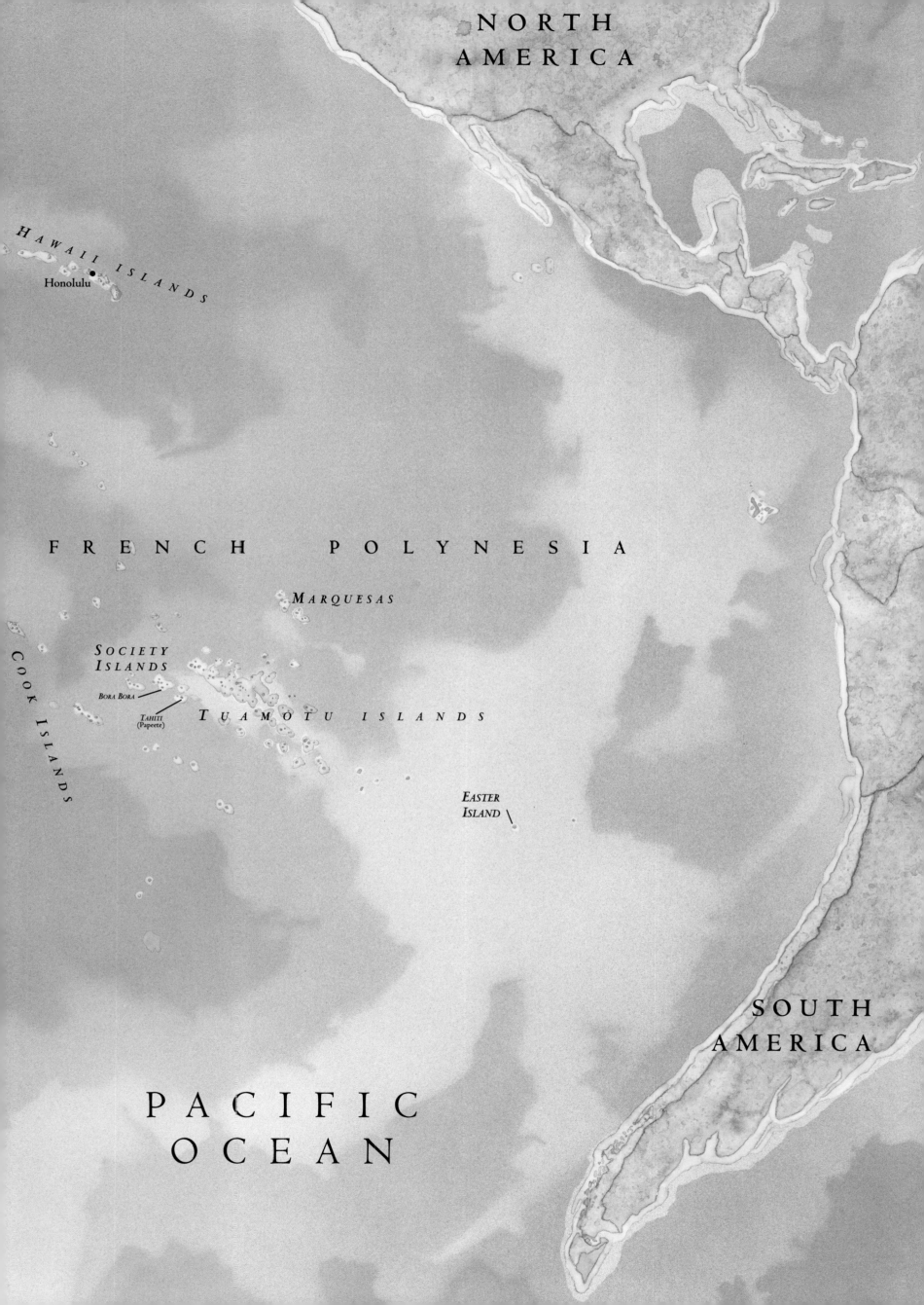

NORTH
AMERICA

HAWAII ISLANDS

Honolulu

FRENCH   POLYNESIA

MARQUESAS

*SOCIETY
ISLANDS*

BORA BORA

TAHITI
(Papeete)

TUAMOTU   ISLANDS

COOK Islands

*EASTER
ISLAND*

SOUTH
AMERICA

PACIFIC
OCEAN

A collection of stunning photographs leads us through the Southern Seas, the domain of myth and dreams. It flies us over the marvellous play of colors of the Polynesian and Micronesian atolls. It takes us diving in coral seas populated by thousands of fish, molluscs and micro-organisms of the most diverse shapes and sizes. It lowers us into the depths of volcanoes and guides us along the Ring of Fire surrounding the Pacific Ocean to illustrate the geological history of the islands' formation. It explores the wild, rain-forest covered mountains of Melanesia. It traverses the infinite deserts of the Australian outback. It describes Oceania, the last continent to be reached by the European colonists, the least densely populated, but the one covering the greatest area. The Pacific Ocean is, in fact, the largest geographical entity on the planet, covering over a third of the surface of the globe. Oceania unfolds as we follow the route of the earliest European navigators searching for *Terra Australis Incognita*, the continent that in the collective eighteenth century imagination should have occupied much of the southern Pacific. We then set sail with the likes of Abel Tasman, Jacob Roggeveen, Samuel Wallis, Louis-Antoine Bougainville, James Cook, Jean François La Pérouse and Joseph Antoine Bruni d'Entrecasteux to discover the customs, beliefs and traditions of the people that lived from Australia to the myriad fragments of land floating in the infinite blue of the Pacific Ocean. Structured as a long voyage among the world's most beautiful islands, this book investigates, with spectacular photos and in-depth texts, the

*I*NTRODUCTION

various pieces making up the complex jigsaw of the Southern Seas. An insular continent in which the primitive ethnic groups of New Guinea live along side the modern and extremely advanced societies of present-day Australia, New Zealand and Hawaii. A reality that includes the dreamlike totemic geography of the Australian Aboriginals and the towering skyscrapers of Honolulu, the mystery of the *moai* of Easter Island and Coober Pedy, the underground city of opal miners, Tonga, the last absolute monarchy in Polynesia and New Zealand, the land of pioneering social reforms that invented the welfare state and first gave the vote to women in 1893. The myths, rituals, dances, sculptures and tattoos of some of the most sharply contrasting peoples on Earth act as counterpoints to the tourist resorts of Bora Bora, the setting for honeymoons and gossip column scoops, made famous by numerous Hollywood films and the Polynesian marriage of Marlon Brando. The voyage begins in Polynesia, the "Garden of Eden" described by the first European explorers, the legendary setting of the *Mutiny of the Bounty* and the paradisical islands painted by Paul Gauguin and recounted in the novels of Robert Louis Stevenson, Herman Melville, Pierre Loti, Mark Twain, Jack London and Somerset Maugham. Their books provide remarkable testimony to the lifestyles and social conditions of these islands, brought together by language and customs, but disseminated within a vast triangle crossing both hemispheres with tips at New Zealand, the Hawaiian archipelago and Easter Island archipelagos that today are very different one from another. While in the Hawaiian Islands, a futuristic All-American society, native Polynesians account for less than one percent of the population, and the *hula* dance has become the exotic calling card of an industry attracting seven million tourists every year, ancient traditions still survive in Tonga and Samoa. The dreamy Kingdom of Tonga still features the social structure of pre-colonial Polynesia, with the sovereign and the court nobles, with precise codes and customs in spite of the arrival of cars, television and the telecommunications industries ranging from satellite TV to one of the most well known Internet providers. Western Samoa, instead, the cradle of the Maori civilization, is isolated from the major international tourist routes and remains the

guardian of Polynesian tradition with a society still based firmly on the *aiga* or extended family, with the majority of the population living in *fale*, huts of wood and palm fronds with no walls. Polynesia also features the isolated Cook Islands, served by beaten-up mail boats that, with breathtaking anchorages and epic delays, hark back to the maritime adventures narrated by Joseph Conrad. The harsh beauty of the Marquesas Islands, crowned by mountain peaks and buried in dripping jungle, the islands of the *recherche sauvage* in which restless spirits such as the French painter Paul Gauguin and the Belgian singer-songwriter Jacques Brel ended their days. The monumentality of Easter Island, studded with hundreds of anthropomorphic statues and integrated with the Hispanic culture of Chile to which it belongs. The turquoise lagoons of the Tuamotu archipelago, of which only from the sky can one fully appreciate the panoramic wonders of the long, narrow coral rings that encircle lagoons pulsating with life. And then there is New Zealand where the sculptures and tattoos of the most numerous Maori population characterize a modern western society that has developed on two islands studded with hundreds of active volcanoes and mountain ranges reminiscent of the European Alps. New Zealand is the country of the world's most famous sailing skippers such as Peter Blake who in the last ten years has triumphed in the America's Cup and the Whitbread round-the-world race. Sailing across the Pacific we reach Micronesia, the world's most Lilliputian region composed of over two thousand splinters of land that placed together would only cover an area equivalent to the smallest European province. Archipelagos straddling the equator, midway between Hawaii and the Philippines with celebrated names such as Marianas, Caroline and Marshall Islands. The theatre of battles between the Japanese and the Americans during the Second World War. Aircraft, tanks, trucks and miscellaneous equipment still lie amidst the coral of the Truk lagoon (Eastern Caroline Islands), forming an authentic submarine war museum. The great attraction of Micronesia are, however, the rock islands of Palau, hundreds of hilly islets covered with tropical vegetation that seem to float on the surface of the turquoise waters. From the dream islands of Micronesia to the inaccessible mountains of New Guinea, the wildest island on Earth, covered with rain-forests, cloaked in mist and inhabited by myriad ethnic groups including Black peoples, Papuans and Pygmies. Stone Age tribes, some of

whom still live in trees and huts built on stilts. New Guinea was the cradle of the Melanesian peoples of Fiji, Vanuatu, the Solomon Islands and New Caledonia. In the Fijian archipelago, the smiling islands, the customs and physical characteristics of the *negritos* have been amalgamated with those of the Polynesians, creating an original culture and one of the gentlest peoples in Oceania. In the late nineteenth century, Fijian rituals were combined with the perfume of curry spices after the British colonizers of the archipelago introduced thousands of Indian immigrants to work in the sugarcane plantations. Thus today Fiji has a multi-racial society with half of the population being of Indian origin. In New Caledonia, the Melanesian Kanak people instead integrated with the French colonists.

New Caledonia, like Tahiti and its islands, is a French overseas territory, the last European colonies in the Pacific. The Vanuatu and Solomon Islands archipelagos are instead ethnically more homogeneous and linked to the traditions and customs of Melanesia. An initiation ritual practiced by the adolescents of Vanuatu, a leap into thin air with the ankles secured by lianas, has inspired the sport of bungee jumping which uses an elastic cord. The Solomon Islands, a theatre of the war in the Pacific, instead inspired the American writer James Michener's *Tales of the South Pacific*, the book for which he was awarded the Pulitzer Prize in 1948. On the south-west side of the Pacific, almost as a bulwark to its immensity, extends Australia, the world's largest island, an extraordinary blend of tribal rituals and glass and concrete skyscrapers, deserts and jungle, mountains and coral reefs. A nation built by convicts and immigrants that, in the collective European imagination, means a land of opportunity in which fortunes are waiting to be made and there is space for all. With just over 18 million inhabitants in a territory as vast as the United States (less Alaska), Australia is one of the nations with the lowest demographic density at just two inhabitants per square mile. A land in which underground mineral reserves provide almost half of the gross national product, education and services are of European standards, bureaucracy is reduced to a minimum and the relationship between salaries and essential goods is more favorable than in Europe. In the country with the greatest variety of beaches in the world, 95% of the population live less than an hour's drive from the sea, the majority in detached houses surrounded by gardens. The World Bank ranks Australia as the world leader in terms of per capita wealth, taking into consideration natural resources, environmental conditions and the quality of life. This is why Sydney, boosted by the Olympic games in the year 2000, heads the list of places in which people would prefer to start a new life. Beyond the metropolis lies the outback, the remote interior with rocks that change color with the passing hours, bizarre local fauna, the rough and solitary lifestyles of the ranchers and the sacred Aboriginal rituals; there is a continent modelled, according to the Aboriginal creation myth, by ancestors who appeared in the guise of birds, serpents and kangaroos.

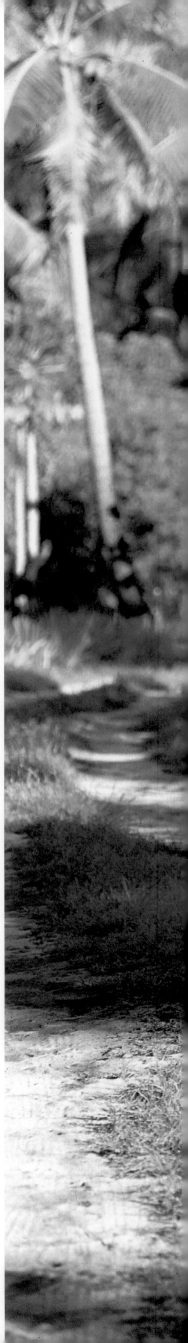

12 top Due to the torrid climate, Polynesian women are accustomed to wearing just a pareo, but on Sundays they dress up and on many islands cover their hair with delightful hats when they go to mass, where the traditional Christian ritual is combined with Maori songs.

12 bottom The face of this woman from Nuku Hiva reveals the racial melting pot that has given origin to the present-day inhabitants of the Marquesas Islands, the northernmost archipelago of French Polynesia, where over two centuries the Mahoi people have mixed with Europeans, Americans and Chinese.

12-13 A boy on horseback in the interior of Lifuka, the principal island of Ha'apai, the central archipelago of the Kingdom of Tonga composed of 54 islands; a serpent of seven coralline fragments surrounded by atolls and by the volcanoes Kao and Tofua.

13 New Guinea has one of the world's most complex ethnic and linguistic profiles, with 240 languages being spoken in Irian Jaya and 769 in Papua New Guinea. The island was populated around 50,000 years ago by hunter-gatherers from South-east Asia.

14-15 This photo reveals the structure of the island of Bora Bora, one of the Society Islands, a typical Pacific atoll. The land in the center is what remains of a volcano. The ring enclosing the lagoon is composed of motus, the coral reefs that have emerged above sea level and have been made fertile by guano and coconuts carried in by the sea.

The Southern Seas represented the final frontier in the European exploration of the globe. For centuries they remained a mysterious region, the source of fabulous myths such as that of *Terra Australis Incognita*, an immense continent that in the collective seventeenth- and eighteenth-century imagination was thought to occupy much of the South Pacific. The Portuguese of the era of the great *descobrimentos* were the first Europeans to land in Oceania. Early in the sixteenth century, exploring the route between India (reached by Vasco da Gama in 1498) and Japan, a number of Lusitanian navigators sighted the northern coast of Australia. In 1519, the Portuguese navigator Ferdinand Magellan fitted out a fleet of five ships and set sail across the Atlantic, passing into a new ocean by way of the strait between South America and Tierra del Fuego which today bears his name. The great sense of tranquility inspired by the deceptive calmness of its waters led him to name this, the stormiest of seas, the Pacific Ocean. A few years earlier, in 1513, the Spaniard Vasco Núñez de Balboa had sighted the great ocean from the Isthmus of Panama and had defined it as the Southern Sea, in contrast with the Caribbean, once known as the North Sea.

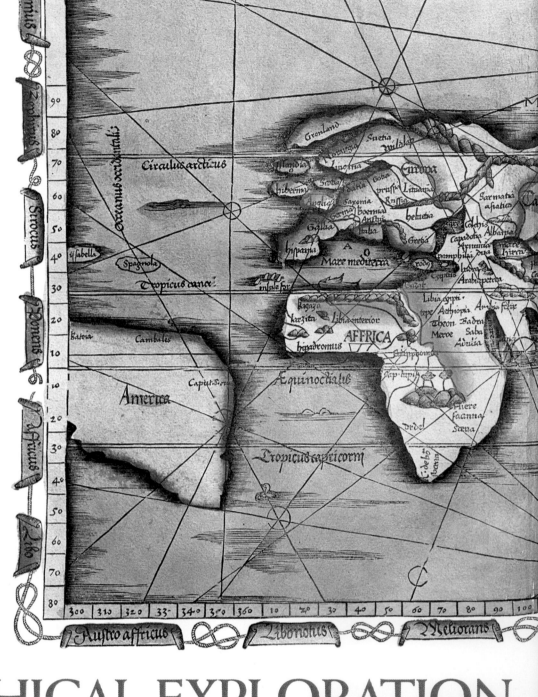

THE FINAL FRONTIER OF GEOGRAPHICAL EXPLORATION

16-17 Waldeemüller's map of the world, published in the 1522 edition of Ptolomy's "Geographia," illustrates the contemporary conception of the world. In the year in which Magellan crossed the Pacific geographers were still unaware of the existence of Australia and of the Oceanic islands.

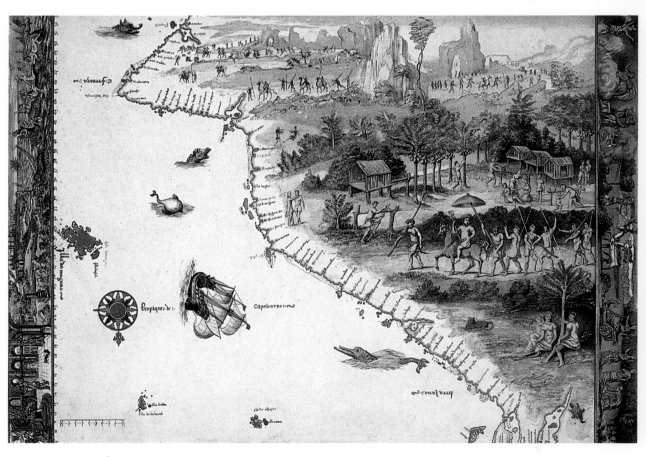

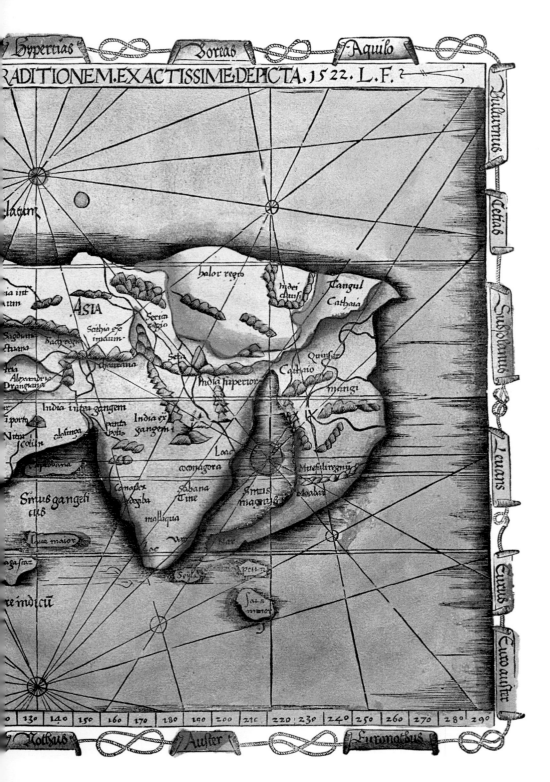

17 top The aristocratic navigator Vasco da Gama, seen here in a portrait from a Portuguese manuscript, opened the way for the exploration of Asia. Actually he was the first European to reach India by sea leaving Lisbon on July 8, 1497 and reaching the Asian subcontinent in May 1498. The Portuguese reached Ceylon in 1506, Malaysia and Sumatra in 1509, the Moluccas in 1512, Macao in 1513, and Nagasaki in 1543.

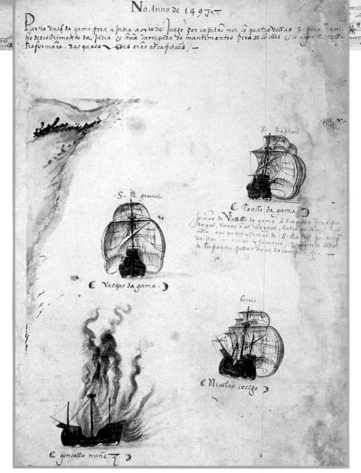

16 bottom This peculiar map drawn in 1547 by Nicholas Vallard depicts Australia, an unexplored continent named Greater Java at the time. After the Dutch navigator Willem Janszoon's landing on the Cape York Peninsula in 1606, the island continent was renamed New Holland; however, its exploration and the penetration of the interior only began two centuries later.

17 bottom Vasco da Gama's fleet, as well as opening the way to the Far East, provided the first hint of the existence of Australia, the coastline of which was observed early in the sixteenth century by Lusitanian ships on the route between India and Japan. According to historians in Lisbon, the Lusitanians also made a number of landings.

Magellan followed the coast of South America through the lower latitudes and, having reached the 30th parallel south, he struck a course north-west until he landed on Puka-Puka, an atoll in the eastern Tuamotu Archipelago. He proceeded beyond the equator and reached Guam, the largest island in Micronesia, and the island of Cebu in the Philippines where he was killed on April 27, 1521. His companions returned to Spain the following year, having circumnavigated the globe for the first time. In 1542, the Spanish organized a naval expedition between Mexico and the Moluccas, in Indonesia. They landed in the Hawaiian archipelago but considered the islands to be of no interest as there was no gold. They subsequently established a naval base on Guam, the largest island in Micronesia, a region over which they retained control until the late nineteenth century. It was the search for the mythical treasure of King Solomon that led the *conquistadores* to the discovery of the islands of the Southern Seas. Alvaro Mendaña left Peru in 1567, heading towards New Guinea. He was to discover an archipelago populated by black-skinned natives that he named the Solomon Islands, convinced they concealed the mythical treasure of the biblical king. On his return to Peru, Mendaña equipped a new fleet and, in 1595, returned to the Solomon Islands intent on colonizing them. He followed a route further to the north and passed through a harsh volcanic archipelago he named the Marquesas Islands, in honour of the consort of Don Garcia Huntado de Mendoza, the Viceroy of Peru and the expedition's financier. Mendaña's landing on the island of Tahuata resulted in the first tragic episode in the history of the relationships between the European colonizers and the Polynesians. His men, incapable of communicating with the Marquesas natives, resorted to an unprovoked massacre. Having reached the Solomon Islands, the attempt to subject them to the rule of the Spanish crown failed, with many of the fleet's crew members being killed in the battles with the natives. Mendaña himself died of malaria. Spain refused to surrender interest in the area and in 1605 Pedro Fernando de Quiros explored the Tuamotu archipelago and discovered the Melanesian archipelago of Vanuatu, while in 1607 Luis Vaez de Torres negotiated the strait between Cape York, in Australia, and New Guinea that now bears his name.

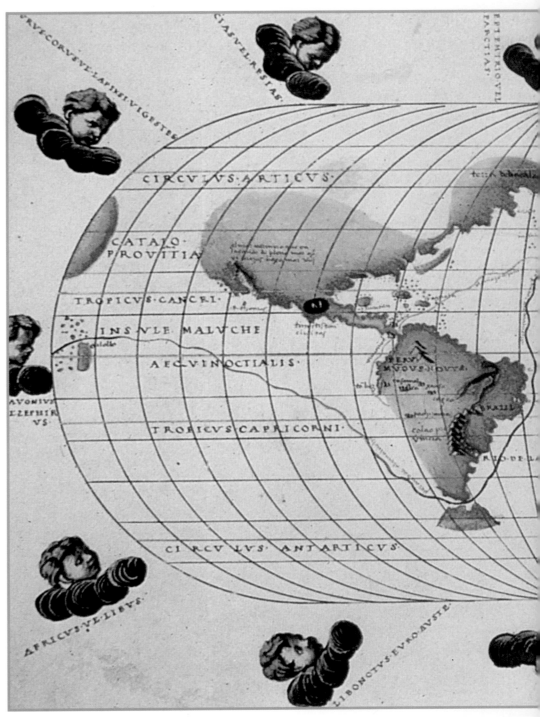

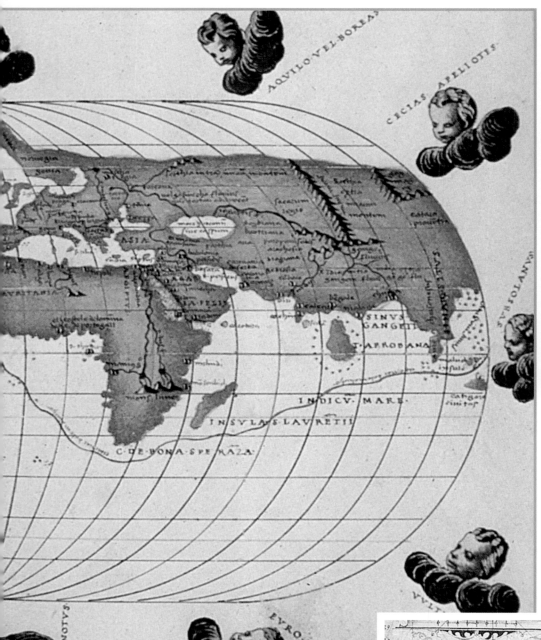

19 top Ferdinand Magellan (1480-1521) was the last of the series of great Portuguese navigators. During a mission financed by Spain in 1519 he searched for a south-west passage to the Orient and, via the strait that today bears his name, discovered the Pacific.

19 bottom The cartographic illustration published in the 1556 edition of "Cosmographie Universelle" by Guillame Le Testu, shows a Terra Australis which the legends of the time claimed was fertile. It was the Dutchman Willem Janszoon who in 1606 discovered the aridity of northern Australia.

18-19 A planisphere illustrating Magellan's 1519-1522 voyage during which he discovered a new ocean that he baptized the Pacific due to its apparently calm waters. The navigator was killed in the Philippines but his companions returned to Spain, circumnavigating the globe for the first time.

18 bottom Magellan set sail from San Lucar with a fleet of five ships and crossed the Atlantic without difficulty. The dangers and discomfort caused by the cold and the currents of the lower latitudes, however, provoked revolts on board; one ship sank and the crew of another mutinied and returned to Spain. This 16th century engraving by De Bry depicts a veritable "rain" of flying fish alongside a ship.

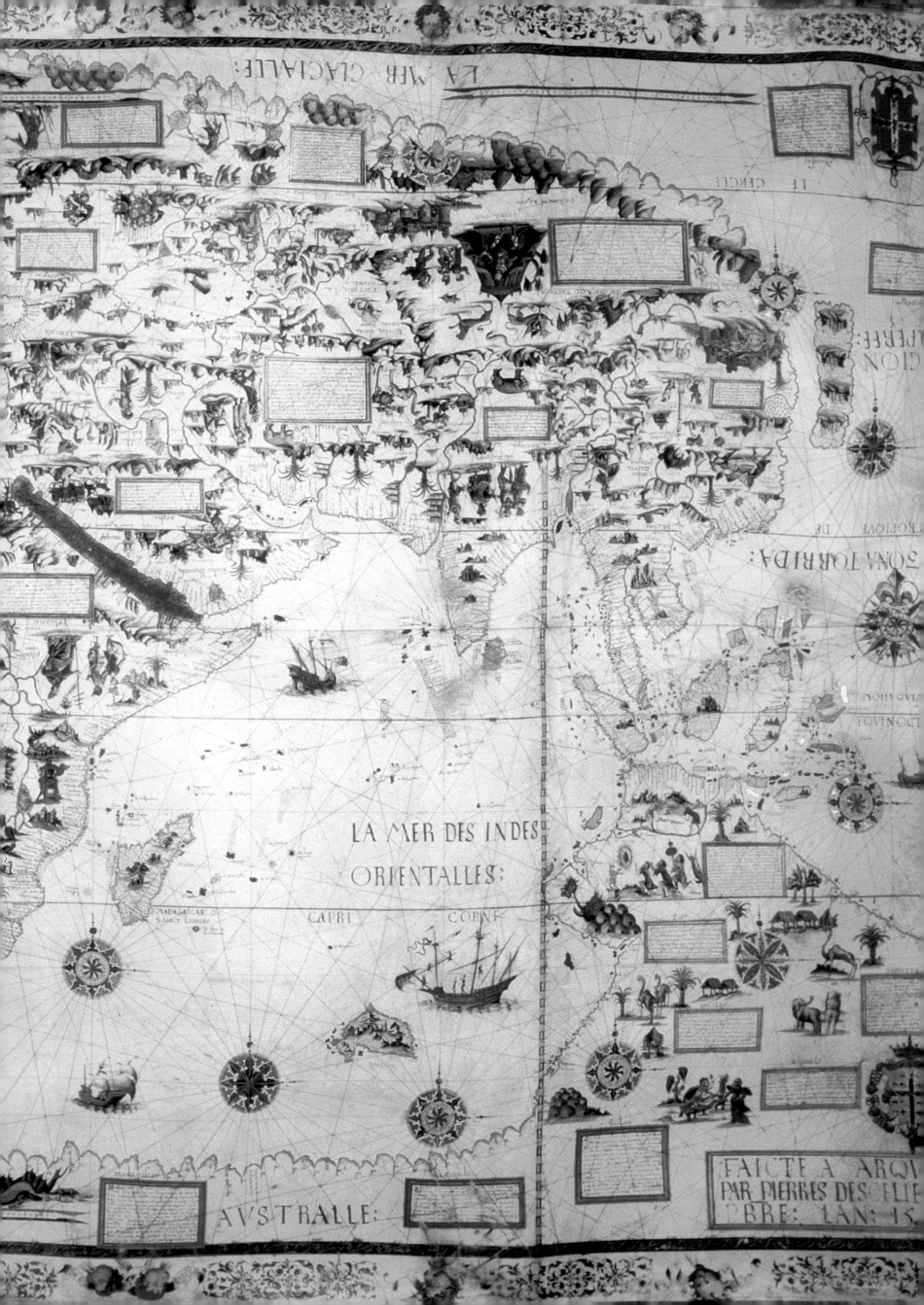

In the meantime, Spanish supremacy in the Pacific had been challenged by the famous English seaman Francis Drake who had passed through the Strait of Magellan in 1577 and, in three years, had completed the first British circumnavigation of the globe. He then returned to the Southern Seas and terrorized the Spanish galleons. In the seventeenth century the British were joined by the Dutch who had created their empire of the East Indies, from Sri Lanka to the islands of present-day Indonesia. In 1606 Willem Janszoon became the first European to land in Australia, the territory being baptized New Holland. While searching for spices, Jansz reached Cape York from Java, but was disappointed in what he found, describing a desert land populated by "primitive Blacks". In 1615, Jacob Lemaire and Willem Schouten completed the first Dutch circumnavigation of the globe and discovered the Polynesian archipelago of Tonga, where they repelled the native attacks with cannon-fire.

In 1616 Dirk Hartog explored the western Australia coast.

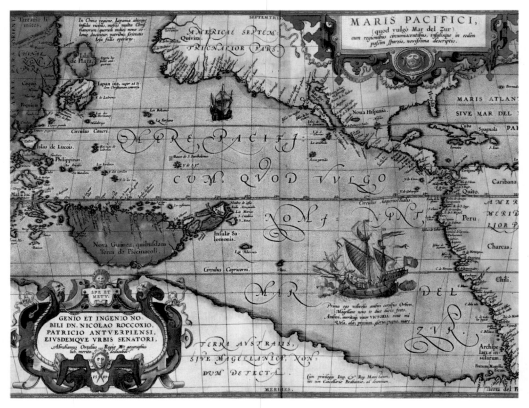

20 Drawn in 1550 by Pierre Desceliers, this map illustrates the Orient in the light of the Portuguese geographical discoveries. It shows Japan, reached in 1543, the Philippines discovered by Magellan in 1521, and the northern coast of Australian sighted by the Portuguese ships.

21 top A map engraved on copper illustrating the hypothetical location of Terra Australis Incognita, an hypothesis disproved by the Englishman James Cook during his second voyage (1772-1775) when he circumnavigated Antarctica and combed much of the southern Pacific.

21 bottom This map from 1570 shows Terra Australis Incognita, a continent as immense as it was mysterious, that in the imagination of contemporary scientists occupied most of the South Pacific.

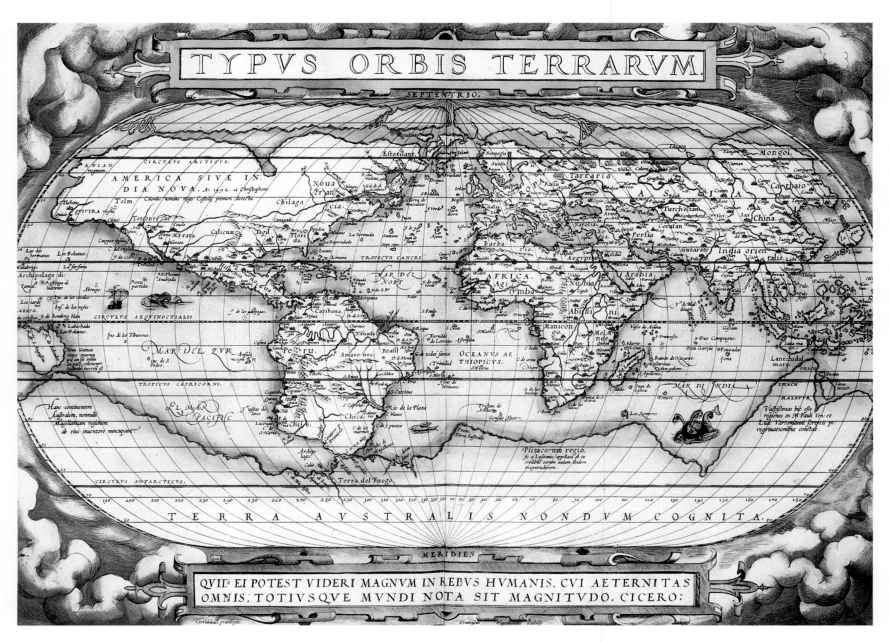

22 top *The famous British seaman Sir Francis Drake passed through the Strait of Magellan in 1577, and in three years completed the first British circumnavigation of the globe. He then returned to the Southern Seas to torment the Spanish galleons and bring an end to Spanish supremacy in the Pacific.*

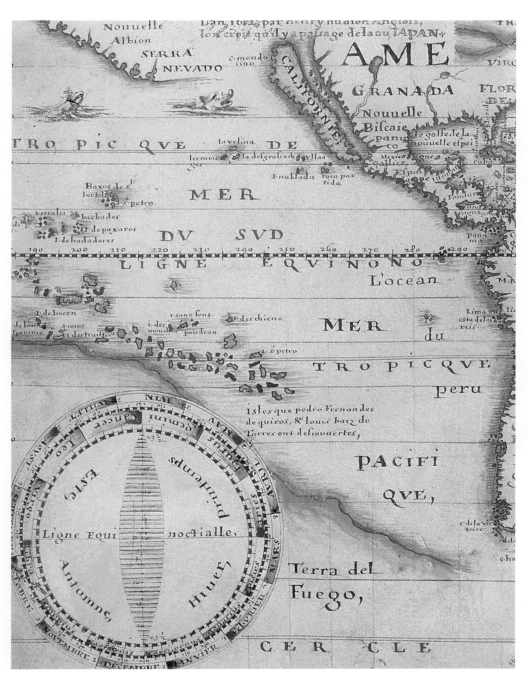

22 bottom *Drawn in 1634 by Jean Guerand, this map shows the islands discovered in the previous century between the Equator and Terra Australis Incognita; the Marquesas and the Solomon Islands discovered by Mendaña in 1567, the Tuamotu archipelago by de Quiros in 1605 and Tonga by Lemaire in 1615.*

22-23 *Drawn a full century after Magellan's voyage, this 1622 map demonstrates the paucity of European knowledge of the Pacific; in spite of the discoveries made by the Spaniard Mendaña, the Portuguese de Quiros, and the Dutchmen Lemaire and Schouten, not a single archipelago is indicated.*

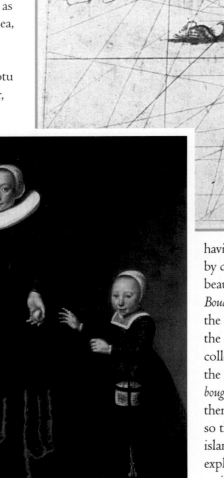

Abel Tasman left Batavia, the present-day Jakarta, in search of the legendary *Terra Australis* in 1642. He skirted the coastline of western Australia—an area already partially explored by Hartog—and discovered Van Diemen's Land (now named Tasmania after its discoverer) before reaching New Zealand, where his attempts to land were thwarted by bands of aggressive Maoris. Tasman was convinced that he had found the west coast of *Terra Australis Incognita* and named it New Zealand after the Dutch region of Zeeland. He therefore headed towards Tonga and circumnavigated Fiji before returning to Batavia (although not aware of the fact, he was actually the first man to sail around Australia).

It was in the eighteenth century that the geographical discoveries in the Pacific coincided with the great European powers' desire for colonial expansion and produced—thanks to the naturalists and illustrators who joined the expeditions—the greatest contribution ever made to our knowledge of the Earth's biological diversity. On Easter day, 1722, the Dutchman Jacob Roggeveen landed on Rapa Nui, which he rebaptized as Easter Island, before proceeding to Vanuatu and New Guinea, where he was repelled by the bellicose natives. In 1767, the Englishman Samuel Wallis landed on Tahiti, established friendly relations with its inhabitants and visited the Tuamotu archipelago and Pentecost Island (Vanuatu). It was, however, the Frenchman Louis-Antoine de Bougainville, who after

having landed on Tahiti in 1768, established the Polynesian myth by drawing parallels between the luxuriant islands populated by beautiful, contented natives and the Garden of Eden. The *Boudeuse*, one of the Bougainville expedition's two ships, carried the naturalist and botanist Philibert Commerson who, during the round-the-world voyage lasting three years (1766-1769), collected and drew hundreds of plants, among which was one of the most famous Oceanic flowering shrubs, which he named *bougainvillaea* after the expedition leader. The French navigator then claimed Tahiti for France and took a Polynesian on board so that he could take one of the inhabitants of these magnificent islands back to Europe along with his plant specimens. He then explored the Samoan archipelago and part of Melanesia, where an island to the East of New Guinea carries his name to this day.

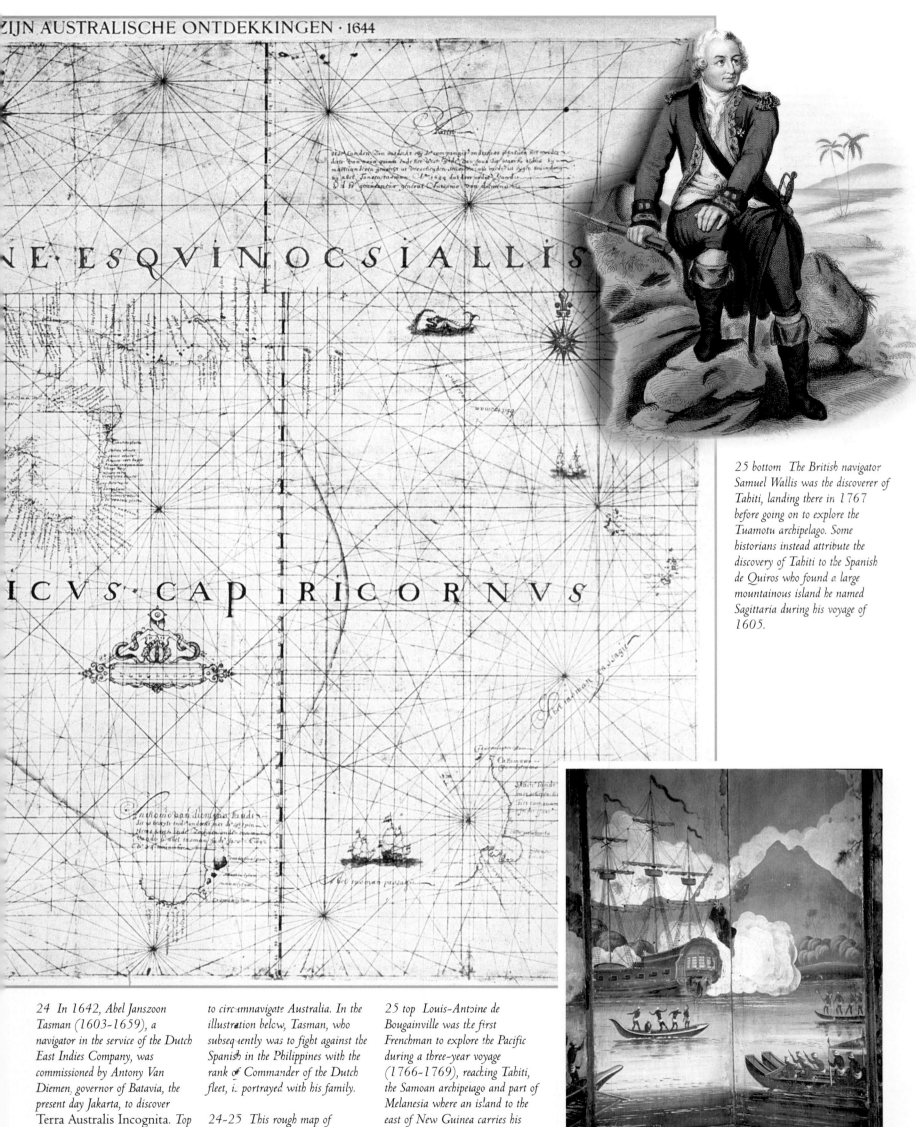

NE·ESQVINOCSIALLIS

ICVS·CAP·RICORNVS

25 bottom The British navigator Samuel Wallis was the discoverer of Tahiti, landing there in 1767 before going on to explore the Tuamotu archipelago. Some historians instead attribute the discovery of Tahiti to the Spanish de Quiros who found a large mountainous island he named Sagittaria during his voyage of 1605.

Captain WALLIS attacked in the Dauphin by the Otahitians.

24 In 1642, Abel Janszoon Tasman (1603-1659), a navigator in the service of the Dutch East Indies Company, was commissioned by Antony Van Diemen, governor of Batavia, the present day Jakarta, to discover Terra Australis Incognita. Top left is a page from Tasman's diary showing a Polynesian canoe. The navigator came into conflict with the Maoris on the coast of New Zealand—which he identified as the mythical continent, passed through the Tongan and Fijian archipelagoes and was the first man to circumnavigate Australia. In the illustration below, Tasman, who subsequently was to fight against the Spanish in the Philippines with the rank of Commander of the Dutch fleet, is portrayed with his family.

24-25 This rough map of Australia was drawn in 1644 by the Dutch navigator Abel Janszoon Tasman who, in 1642, followed the coastline of western Australia— along the route already partially explored by Dirk Hartog—and discovered Tasmania without realizing that it was an island.

25 top Louis-Antoine de Bougainville was the first Frenchman to explore the Pacific during a three-year voyage (1766-1769), reaching Tahiti, the Samoan archipelago and part of Melanesia where an island to the east of New Guinea carries his name.

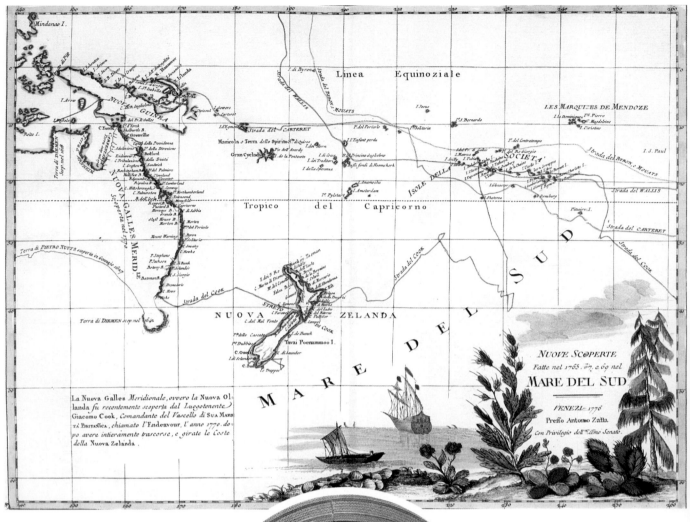

26 top This map shows the British discoveries in the Pacific made between 1765 and 1769. James Cook's route is marked in red, John Byron's in yellow, Philip Carteret's in light green and that of Samuel Wallis in dark green.

26 center As well as having discovered the fertile east coast of Australia, the Englishman James Cook revolutionized navigation with introduction of longitude calculations and the development of a diet capable of defeating scurvy.

26 bottom The Polynesian islanders all used canoes up to 66 feet long, vessels with single or twin hulls (made from tree trunks hollowed-out with axes), and equipped with one or two sails made from woven leaves and rigged with coconut fiber ropes.

26-27 This painting of the Endeavour, Cook's flagship, has passed erroneously into history as depicting the landing in the Friendly Islands (the name given by the Europeans to Tonga), but probably shows the Marquesas Islands, the only archipelago with bays overlooked by such steep mountains.

The voyages of James Cook—the Englishman who changed the course of history in the Pacific—also had scientific as well as political aims. A physician, mathematician, and astronomer as well as a navigator, Cook was accompanied on his first voyage (1768-1771) by the botanists Joseph Banks and Daniel Carl Solander who catalogued hundreds of unknown animal and plant species in Tahiti, New Zealand and Australia. The German naturalist Georg Foster participated in Cook's second voyage (1772-1775) and his book "*A Voyage Round the World*" contained the first anthropological observations regarding the customs of the natives of New Zealand, the Society Islands, Tonga (then known as the Friendly Islands), Rapa Nui, the Marquesas, Vanuatu and New Caledonia, from social organization to sexual practices and cannibalism. The Royal Geographic Society of London financed Cook's first voyage to discover *Terra Australis Incognita* and observe the passage of Venus from Tahiti. In three months; Cook explored the Society Islands, the Tuamotu Archipelago and the Austral Islands. In search of the legendary *Terra Australis*, he then sailed on a south-westerly heading and landed in

27 bottom This drawing, taken from Cook's diary, shows the tattooed face of a Maori of New Zealand where the men decorated their faces, thighs and buttocks with curvilinear motifs by cutting the skin with pig's teeth and colouring the incisions with fossil carbon dye.

27

New Zealand where he circumnavigated and mapped the
two islands separated by the strait named after him.
Heading north-west and crossing the Tasman Sea on the
April 28, 1770, he reached an inlet rich in unknown plants
on the south-east coast of Australia—a few dozen miles
south of present-day Sydney—which he baptized Botany
Bay and laid claim to the new land on behalf of the British
crown. Cook then sailed north along the coast, sighted the
great bay where the city of Sydney now stands and named it
Port Jackson, and then encountered the Great Barrier reef
on which his ship the *Endeavour* ran aground. In order to
repair the ship he was forced to spend seven weeks on the
coast, establishing the first (albeit temporary) white
settlement in Australia where Cooktown, a city founded by
gold miners in 1873, now stands. Having set sail once
again, Cook landed on Lizard Island where, from the hill
dominating the island, he was able to observe the
tremendous undertow generated by the Great Barrier Reef
for first time. On his return to London, Cook was unable
to convince the British admiralty that the mythical southern
land much larger than Australia did not exist and he was sent
back to the Pacific in 1772. During this second voyage the

28 top *A drawing depicting the
landing of James Cook on
Erromango in the New Hebrides
(Vanuatu), an island populated
by cannibals. Some decades after
Cook's passage, John Williams, the
London Missionary Society's chief
officer in the Pacific, was killed
and eaten here.*

28-29 This drawing from the rich collection of illustrations in James Cook's travel atlas, depicts a twin-hulled canoe typical of the Hawaiian Islands. A twin-hulled canoe from the Hawaiian archipelago, baptized as the Sandwich Islands by James Cook, during his second voyage in honour of the First Lord of the Admiralty, John Montague, Earl of Sandwich.

29 top This drawing depicts an inhabitant of Tanna, one of the southernmost islands of the Vanuatu archipelago peopled by Melanesians who still today practice initiation rites with dances, circumcisions, the killing of pigs and face painting during the Nekowiar celebrations.

29 bottom Portrayed here, the landing of James Cook in the Vanuatu archipelago (then known as the New Hebrides) took place during his second voyage (1772-1775) around the world when he explored many of the Pacific archipelagos.

28 bottom left This contemporary drawing depicts Poulaho, the King of Tonga at the time of Cook's landing on Tongatapu (during his second Pacific voyage). Cook nicknamed the archipelago the "Friendly Islands" because of the cordiality with which he had been received by its inhabitants.

28 bottom right A masked man from the Hawaiian Islands, portrayed in 1779 by John Webber, the English illustrator who accompanied Cook during his third and last Pacific voyage. The Hawaiians boasted the most highly decorated ornaments in the whole of Polynesia.

30 top   The native Tahitian fleet, as seen in this plate from Cook's travel atlas, was composed of twin-hulled canoes with a broad central platform. This type of vessel, found throughout eastern Polynesia, is propelled by two sails hoisted on twin masts.

30 bottom   This contemporary drawing shows the preparations for a human sacrifice on Tahiti where Cook reported having seen an altar decorated with forty-nine skulls. Ritual homicide was common to the whole of Polynesia where war canoes were launched on the bodies of virgin girls.

explorer circumnavigated Antarctica and explored much of the South Pacific, disproving once and for all the myth of the mysterious continent. During this voyage he explored the archipelagos of the Cook Islands, Tonga, Fiji, Vanuatu, New Caledonia, the Marquesas Islands and the Society Islands as well as Easter Island. He also reached Hawaii which he baptized the Sandwich Islands in honor of the First Lord of the Admiralty and his patron, John Montagu, Earl of Sandwich. On Hawaii, as he recorded in his log, Cook was the first European to observe the Polynesians riding the gigantic ocean waves balancing on wooden boards up to 17 feet long, the original surfers, practitioners of a sport that over the centuries has become the most popular in the Pacific.

Cook's explorations were concluded in the Hawaiian Islands during his third Pacific voyage. Initially the natives considered the English captain to be a god, partly because he had by chance landed on Hawaii during the annual ceremony dedicated to a Polynesian deity. Irritated by the habits of the white men, however, they soon changed their minds. On the occasion of his third landing on February 14, 1779, they killed and probably ate the captain, his companions only managing to recover his cranium after it had been carefully scalped, according to a local tradition. Thus died one of the greatest explorers in history. As well as having discovered the fertile east coast of Australia and intuited the potential of a land that had until then been considered barren and inhospitable, Cook revolutionized navigation and cartography, introducing longitudinal calculation and developing a diet capable of defeating scurvy.

30-31 A contemporary drawing depicting the nocturnal dance of the women of the Ha'apai archipelago (Tonga), one of the Oceanic countries in which dance is still today the most vibrant form of artistic expression and traditional dances are taught in state schools.

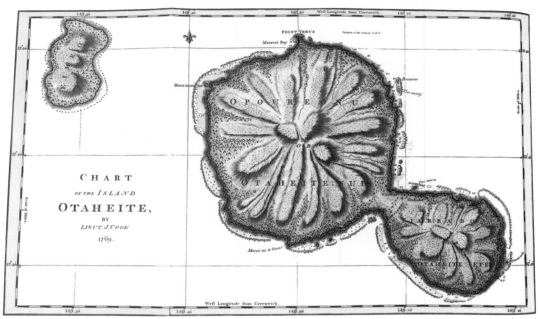

CHART
OF THE ISLAND
OTAHEITE,
BY
LIEUT. J. COOK
1769.

31 top A drawing of Oto, the sovereign of Tahiti at the time of Cook's landing. Tahitian society was divided into three classes, the ariki (the tribal chieftains whose authority derived from spiritual power), the rangatira (a form of land-owning aristocracy) and the ordinary people.

31 bottom This map of Tahiti was drawn in 1769 by James Cook on the occasion of his first Pacific voyage, when he was commissioned by the Royal Geographic Society of London to discover Terra Australis Incognita and to observe the passage of Venus from Tahiti.

31

33 top left This drawing portrays a native Polynesian from the Cook Islands located to the west of Tahiti. The English captain landed in the archipelago in 1773 during his second Pacific voyage and named it the Harvey Islands in honor of the Earl of Bristol.

33 top righ. A portrait of a Maori from New Zealand where in the thirteenth century the Polynesians abandoned the art of navigation and developed a civilization of warrior farmers and, thanks to the immense interior of the country, enjoyed the greatest demographic expansion in the Pacific area.

33 bottom Joseph Banks and Daniel Carl Solander, naturalists on Cook's first voyage, cataloged hundreds of unknown plant and animal species in Tahiti, New Zealand and Australia, as did Georg Foster, the scientist who participated in the second voyage.

32-33 James Cook was killed in the Hawaiian archipelago in 1779 on the occasion of his third voyage. Initially the Hawaiians saw him as a god, but irritated by the customs of the white men, they killed and ate the captain, the English seamen recovering only his cranium.

32 bottom left A portrait of Omai, the Polynesian whom Cook took on board at Raiatea. After having acted as translator at Tonga and Tahiti, Omai reached London, met the king and became an attraction in the capital's salons before returning to Polynesia with Cook on his last voyage.

32 bottom right A pastel portrait of Odaïdi, a young Tahitian taken on board the Resolution by Cook during his third voyage. In the late eighteenth century it became common practice for the British ships sailing in the Pacific to engage Polynesian sailors, as the story of the Bounty demonstrates.

34 top The oil painting "Empire and Science" by Mansiaux shows Jean François de Galaup, Count of La Pérouse, receiving instruction: for the naval expedition to the Pacific from Louis XVI of France. La Pérouse departed from Brest on August 1, 1785.

34 bottom The frontispiece from the atlas accompanying the four-volume account of the voyages of La Pérouse. The atlas contained nautical charts and reproductions of the drawings executed by the naturalists and scientists aboard La Boussole and L'Astrolabe. The documents escaped the loss of the French admiral's ships as La Pérouse had entrusted them to an officer who carried the precious papers home by land.

The French crown, worried that Cook's discoveries gave Britain supremacy in the Pacific, fitted out the ships *La Boussole* and *L'Astrolabe* for an oceanic expedition under the command of Jean François de Galaup, Count of La Pérouse. Setting sail from Brest in Brittany on the 1st of August, 1785, La Pérouse rounded Cape Horn the following year, skirted round South America, visited Hawaii and reached Alaska before exploring the Strait of Sakhalin, descending along the Pacific coast of Chinese and exploring the Philippines, the Marshall Islands, Samoa (where in a skirmish with the Polynesians he lost eleven men), Tonga and Norfolk Island. In 1788, La Pérouse landed at Port Jackson (present-day Sydney) where the British had recently founded a penal colony. From here he despatched a letter and his log-book to Paris, announcing his intention to head north-east to explore Tonga and Melanesia. This was the last that has heard of him and his two ships. During his three-year voyage, La Pérouse had largely completed the geographical exploration of the Pacific, opening the way for western colonization. Following the loss of its American colonies as a consequence of the War of Independence, Britain took Botany Bay into consideration as a new penal colony. In 1788, the English captain Arthur Phillip landed at Port Jackson with a fleet of eleven ships carrying prisoners, soldiers and officers, at total of a thousand persons, the nucleus of white Australia. The new colony got off to a difficult start due to Aboriginal ambushes and experiments with agriculture ill-suited to the environment that were soon the cause of food shortages. A fleet carrying supplies and over two hundred deported women, mostly old and infirm, came to the colony's aid in 1790.

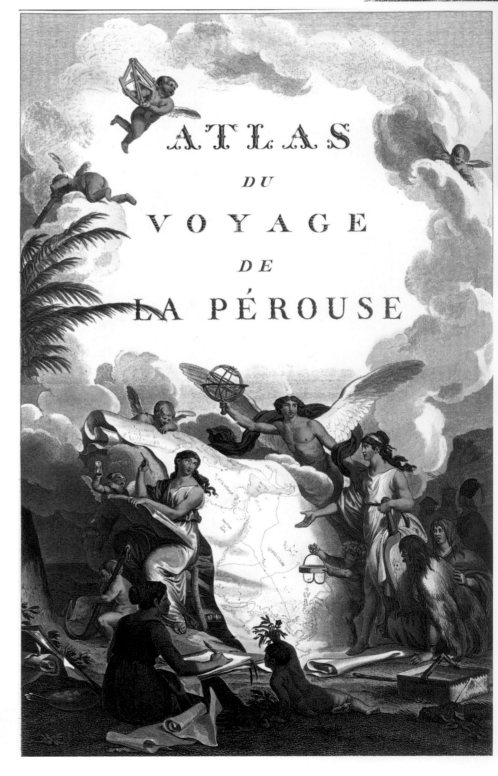

LA PÉROUSE

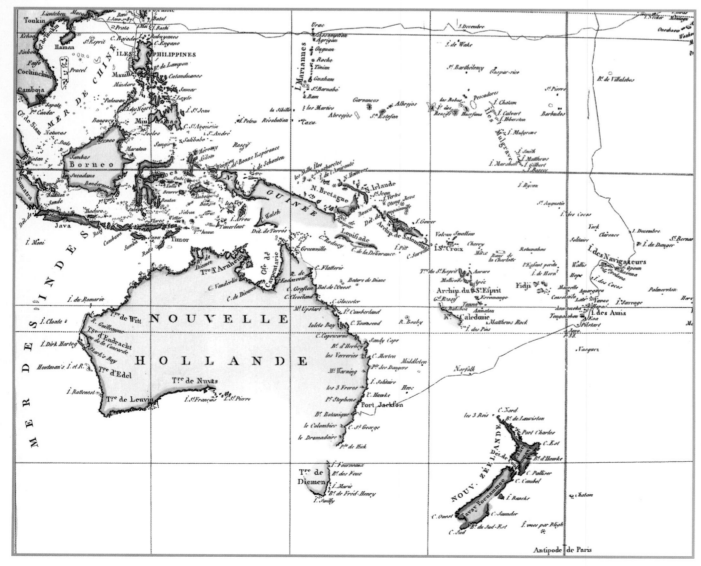

34-35 The French crown fitted out the ships La Boussole and L'Astrolabe and financed the Oceanic voyage of La Pérouse because, following the geographical discoveries made by Cook, it was deeply concerned about Britain's potential supremacy in the Pacific region. This drawing shows the two French frigates surrounded by Polynesian canoes in the waters of an archipelago. The natives were fascinated by the European ships, referring to ancient legends, many thought that the white men were gods that had descended from heavens.

35 bottom La Pérouse visited the Hawaiian Islands, Alaska and the Chinese coast. He explored the Philippines, the Marshall Islands, Samoa, Tonga and Norfolk Island, landed at the site of Sydney and headed north-east to comb Tonga and Melanesia before his ships disappeared without trace.

36 top Taken from La Pérouse's atlas, this drawing shows a canoe used by the inhabitants of Rapa Nui. Having reached the island, the most remote in Polynesia, the Maoris unsuccessfully attempted to migrate further south but lost their seafaring skills and previously infallible sense of orientation.

36 bottom The La Pérouse expedition was equipped with this 1786 map of Easter Island. In the eighteenth century Rapa Nui appeared as a desert island with around two thousand inhabitants living naked and undernourished in the bizarre setting of toppled moai.

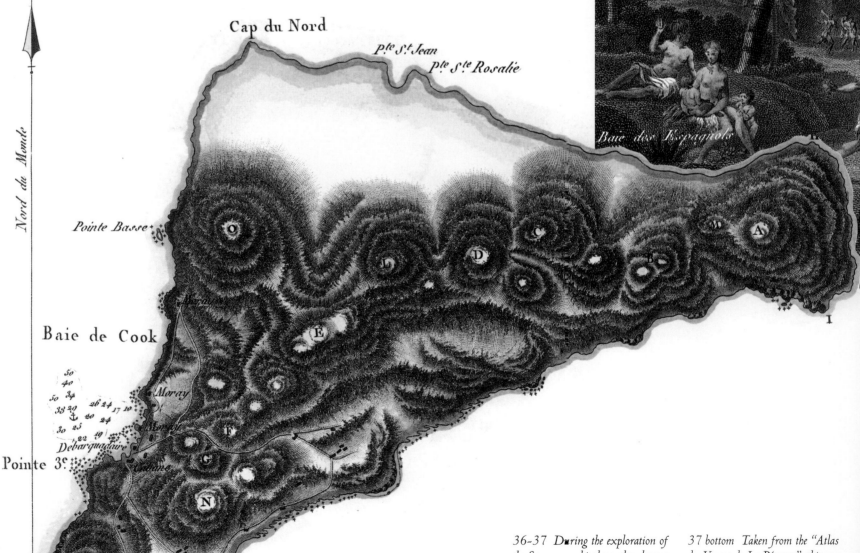

Cap du Nord

P.te S.t Jean

P.te S.te Rosalie

Nord du Monde

Pointe Basse

Baie de Cook

Baie des Espagnols

50
40
50 34   26 24 17 10
33 20   40 24
30 25   19
1 22
Moray
Maro
Debarquadere
Pointe 3.e
Pointe 2.e
Pointe 1.e
Pointe I.e
Piton
Ilot
Cap du Sud-Ouest

O
D
A
E
F
G
N

36-37 During the exploration of the Samoan archipelago, then known as the Navigators Islands, La Pérouse's boats were attacked by Polynesian canoes and in the furious battle that followed eleven of the French expedition's men were killed.

37 bottom Taken from the "Atlas du Voyage de La Pérouse", this engraving shows the French explorers measuring the huge moai of Easter Island. The first Westerner to reach Rapa Nui was the Dutchman, Jacob Roggeveen. He landed on the island on Easter Day, 1722, and named it accordingly.

38-39 This aquatint by Robert Dodd was published in 1790 and depicts one of the most tragic episodes of the most famous mutiny in history: Captain William Bligh, along with a number of his officers and sailors, a total of 18 men, boarding one of the Bounty's small boats. The engraving, today conserved in the National Library of Australia at Canberra, portrays Christian Fletcher, the leader of the revolt on April 28, 1789, in the waters of Tonga.

38 bottom Captain William Bligh, seen here in a portrait hanging in the Mitchell Library in New South Wales, together with a few faithful crew members, sailed no less that 3,618 miles, overcoming numerous difficulties such as an attack by Fijian cannibals. After having reached the Portuguese colony of Timor in Indonesia, he quickly travelled to England where a hunt for the mutineers immediately was organized.

In the meantime, the Pacific had witnessed the most famous mutiny in history, the first great act of insubordination towards the British crown. The story of the *Bounty* predated the French Revolution by just a few months and thus took on symbolic importance. On the one hand, Romanticism elevated the mutineers to the status of revolutionary heroes struggling against tyranny and abuse; on the other, the aristocracy of all Europe saw grave danger in the revolt and London employed all the means at its disposal to capture and hang the rebels in order to reaffirm the authority of the crown and discourage potential emulators.

The *Bounty*, captained by William Bligh, arrived in the Pacific in 1789 to collect bread-fruits to be used to establish British plantations in the Antilles and feed African slaves. Having failed to round Cape Horn due to bad weather, Bligh had chosen to follow the Cape of Good Hope route, reaching Tahiti in the wrong season. While waiting for the fruit to ripen for harvesting, his men devoted themselves to idleness and the attentions of the sensuous Polynesian women. Captain Bligh decided to return to sea but the crew, composed of 45 European and Tahitian volunteers, was no longer willing to submit to the rigid on-board discipline. On April 28, 1789, led by Christian Fletcher, the crew mutinied in the waters of Tonga off the Ha'apai archipelago. Bligh and the eighteen seamen who had remained faithful to him were given a boat and, in the most remarkable feat of rowing in history, they passed through the Fijian archipelago, which he called the "Cannibal Islands" after being attacked by canoes paddled by flesh-eating natives, and 3,618 miles later reached Timor (Indonesia), then a colony of Portugal, a British ally. The crew survived—only one man was lost—by eating fish and sea-birds. On his return to London on March 14, 1790, Bligh triggered a massive hunt for the mutineers. Some were shipwrecked, others were captured and hanged on Tahiti. After wandering the ocean at length, on January 15, 1790, Christian Fletcher and the 14 men and 14 women with him discovered the uninhabited Pitcairn Island, south-east of the Tuamotu archipelago, where they decided to found a community.

Fate was against them, however, and after having scuttled the *Bounty* to avoid second thoughts, a dispute between the European sailors and the Polynesians developed into a massacre. The only survivors were John Adams, nine Tahitian women and a group of children.

39 top This engraving by H. Adlard based on a drawing by R. Beechey, portrays John Adams, one of the mutineers from the Bounty who settled on the uninhabited Pitcairn Island to the south-east of the Tuamotu group. Adams, the only survivor of the group of rebels, was found in the company of a group of Tahitian women and children and was transported to England. He was put on trial and found guilty but was subsequently pardoned. He died in 1829 at the age of 65.

39 bottom This lithograph depicts the village on Pitcairn Island founded by the group of mutineers from the Bounty, led by Christian Fletcher, in 1825. Fletcher, accompanied by 14 men and 14 women, sailed the Polynesian waters for years until, on January 15, 1790, he discovered the small uninhabited island where he decided to found a community. In order to avoid second thoughts, the Bounty was scuttled, but the community did not enjoy good fortune and a violent quarrel between the European sailors and the Polynesian turned into a veritable massacre. When the British finally landed on the island, the only survivor proved to be John Adams.

40 top A water-color showing the brig the Beagle anchored in Sydney bay. The voyage of the Beagle around the world, in which the British naturalist Charles Darwin participated, turned into the most fruitful scientific exploration of the Pacific.

40-41 This map from 1850 shows all of the Pacific archipelagos. Once the naval exploration had been completed, in the middle of the nineteenth century there was intense competition amongst Britain, France, the United States and Germany to colonize Polynesia, Melanesia and Micronesia.

41 bottom A water-color portrait of Charles Darwin who, thanks to the zoological, botanical and paleontologic observations he completed during the Beagle's five-year voyage around the world, was later able to develop his theory of the evolution of species.

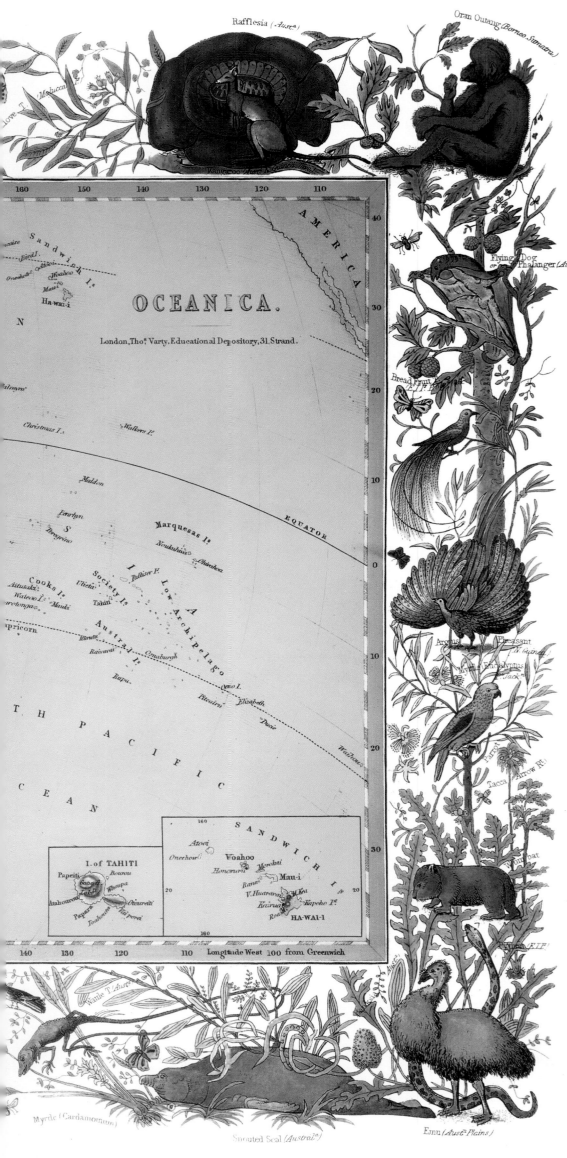

The expedition, led by the Italian Alessandro Malaspina in the service of the Spanish crown, was less romantic than the adventure of the *Bounty*, but much more profitable. In five years (1789-1794) he made advances in the study of the shape of the Earth and brought back to Europe mineral, botanical, zoological and ethnographic samples as well as accurate illustrative documentation of the Oceanic flora.

In 1791, the French prepared the ships *Recherche* and *Espérance* for another Pacific expedition in the wake of La Pérouse. The ships were commanded by Rear Admiral Joseph Antoine Bruni d'Entrecasteaux and carried a team of scientists. The French fleet explored south-western Australia, Tasmania, Tonga, the Solomon Islands and New Caledonia but found no trace of La Pérouse. It then headed for Indonesia where Entrecasteaux died on Java in 1793.

In the meantime, a small group of British seal hunters had established a camp in 1792 in an uninhabited area of New Zealand's South Island, the country's first white settlement, followed a few years later by a whaling community at the Bay of Islands on the north-east coast of North Island. In the late eighteenth century, whaling stations were also established in the Hawaiian archipelago. In 1797, the first pastors of the London Missionary Society landed on Tahiti, an island frequented by sandalwood merchants as well as American whalers. Thus began a process whereby in just a few decades much of Oceania was converted to Christianity at the expense of many aspects of Polynesian culture. Nudity, dancing, sexual permissiveness and tattooing were condemned by the missionaries as impure acts and disappeared from most of Polynesia. Traditional dances and tattooing were only revived after 1970 as expressions of a Maori movement devoted to the reappropriation of native cultural roots.

One of the mysteries of the Pacific was resolved in 1808 when the American ship *Topaz* commanded by Captain Matthew Folger discovered Pitcairn Island and the descendants of the mutineers of the Bounty. John Adams, who in the meantime had transformed himself into a Protestant priest and held bible classes for his descendants, was transported to London where after a trial he was pardoned.

William Bligh, the iron-willed captain of the *Bounty*, had been sent to Sydney as governor in order to restore order to a colony dominated by the miscreants of the Rum Company who imported liquor from Bengal (India). However, Bligh too failed and was relieved of his post in 1808. It was his successor Lachlan Macquarie who was responsible for the reforms that transformed Australia into an attractive destination for free colonists. The worst elements of early Australian society were deported to the new frontier lands of Norfolk Island, Tasmania and Moreton Bay (the site of present-day Brisbane). Within a decade, a plan of works turned Sydney into a true city; the first bank was opened, currency was minted and the exploration of the territory, defined as *terra nullius* or uninhabited (despite the presence of hundreds of thousands of Aboriginals), was encouraged. In 1814, following a suggestion by the navigator Matthew Flinders, the colony adopted the name Australia instead of New Holland. That same year the Reverend Samuel Marsden, well known in Sydney for beating out sins with his whip, opened a mission at Russell with the objective of converting the New Zealand Maoris to Christianity and keeping the European adventurers who frequented the Bay of Island at arm's length. To this end, London extended New South Wales (Sydney) legislation to New Zealand in 1817. In 1826, in order to obstruct French interest in the region, a new colony was founded in western Australia where the city of Perth now stands. That year, a new French expedition set sail from Toulon in search of La Pérouse in the Fijian Islands, where stories were told of the wrecks of two large sailing ships. The expedition was led by Jules Dumont d'Urville, a navigator and scientist who, having rounded the Cape of Good Hope, surveyed the coasts of New Zealand and searched the Tonga archipelago and many of the Melanesian islands, mapping over 2,485 miles of shoreline. The mission failed to find any trace of La Pérouse, however. It was left to Captain Peter Dillion to discover in 1827, proof of the loss of *La Boussole* and *L'Astrolabe* on the rocks of Vanikoro (now known as Santa Cruz) in the Solomon Islands, one of the areas searched by Entrecasteaux during the first expedition sent to look for La Pérouse.

In 1828, the Dutch, present in Indonesia for two centuries, extended their control over the western part of New Guinea, the present-day Indonesian region of Irian Jaya. The exploration of the Australian interior began in 1830 with the journeys of Charles Sturt, who reached the Simpson Desert and navigated the rivers of New South Wales. The most celebrated scientific voyage of discovery in the Pacific got underway in 1831. This was the round-the-world voyage of the *Beagle* in which the English naturalist Charles Darwin participated. Five years (1831-1836) during the course of which Darwin completed botanical, zoological, paleontological and geological observations; an experience recorded in the scientist's diary "*A Naturalist's Voyage*" that allowed him to interpret the geophysical ocean for the first time (from the Ring of Fire to the formation of the atolls), and later to develop his theory of the evolution of species.

Captain William Hobson arrived at the Bay of Islands from Sydney in 1837, charged with reaching an agreement with the Maoris whereby New Zealand would be subjected to the authority of the British crown. In 1340, he signed the Treaty of Waitangi whereby a group of tribal chieftains accepted British sovereignty in return for guarantees regarding tribal lands. This marked the beginning of the colonization of New Zealand. The New Zealand Company, founded in London by Edward Gibbon Wakefield, organized dozens of ships for would-be emigrants, free colonists who left Britain in order to establish farms and exploit the natural riches of the new country. The large-scale arrival of whites sparked off land disputes with the natives that degenerated into the Maori War, which dragged on until 1867, when the Maoris were guaranteed representation in the colonial parliament. In the same period Paris, began to exert control over Tahiti and in 1838, a French frigate obliged Queen Pomare IV to accept a consul. In 1842, taking advantage of internal conflicts among the Polynesian nobility, the French persuaded the tribal chieftains to sign a request for protection. The Leeward Islands became a French protectorate that was extended to include the Marquesas and Tuamotu archipelagos, and, in 1853, a penal colony was founded in New Caledonia. The influence of the United States also

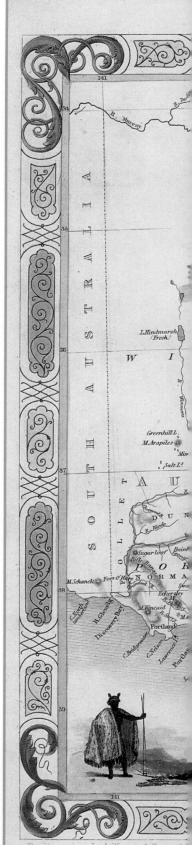

The Illustrations by A. Warren & Engraved

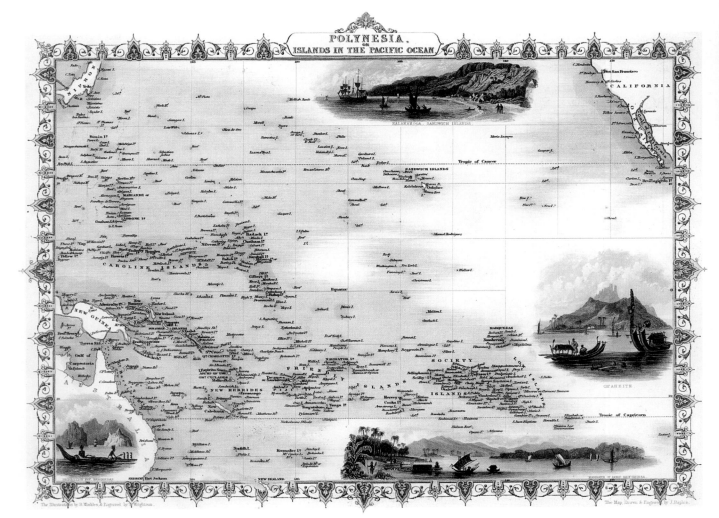

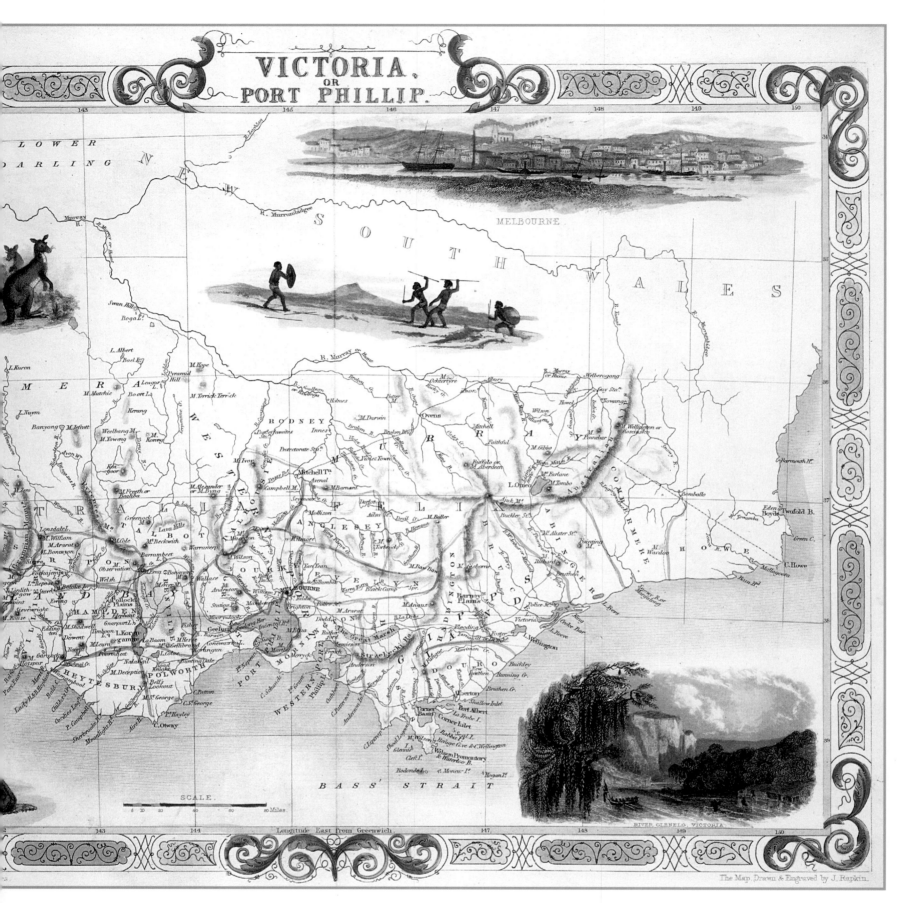

VICTORIA,
OR
PORT PHILLIP.

MELBOURNE.

RIVER GLENELG, VICTORIA.

SCALE.

The Map Drawn & Engraved by J. Rapkin.

began to be felt in the Pacific from 1848. In the Hawaiian Islands, pressure exerted by American traders led King Kamehameha III to abolish collective inheritance of land and to introduce the concept of private property. In the meantime, the exploration of the Australian interior was completed between 1840 and 1862. John Eyre crossed the country on foot from east to west, skirting around the Great Australian Bight, Ludwig Leichhardt opened a trail between Brisbane and Darwin, Edmund Kennedy explored much of the Cape York Peninsula and John McDouall Stuart became the first man to traverse the continent from south to north, covering the almost 1,990 miles that separate Adelaide from Darwin. The Stuart expedition was financed with profits from the gold deposits discovered at Bathurst, New South Wales, in 1851. The discovery of the precious metal revolutionized Australian history as gold fever stimulated the first great migratory wave. After gold-bearing seams were found in Victoria, ships crowded with immigrants from Europe, China and the United States began to dock at Melbourne. In the twelve years between 1851 and 1863, the population of

42 bottom A map from the second half of the nineteenth century combining cartography with illustrations of life in the archipelagos. The exoticism of the Southern Seas, fed by the myths of erotic dances and beautiful women inclined to free love, began to take hold in this period.

42-43 A map from 1849 showing the Australian colony of Victoria, which obtained independence from New South Wales (Sydney) in 1851, following the discovery of gold. The rush to mine the precious metal increased the state's population and transformed Melbourne into a city.

Te raaii rahi

Australia rose from 400,000 to 1,000,000. Melbourne became a city with hotels, theatres, banks, street lighting and luxurious residential quarters. The discovery of deposits of silver, copper and zinc in various regions of the country laid the basis of its future mineralogical power. The transportation of prisoners from Britain ceased in 1868 and the five colonies into which Australia was divided became a normal country. In 1872, 36,000 poles were erected along the trail established by Stuart in order to create a telegraph link between Darwin and the south, already in communication with London via Singapore, Bombay and Aden. In the center of the continent a telegraph station was built around which grew up the town of Alice Springs.

The French occupation of Tahiti accelerated the British

and American plans for the colonization of the Oceanic archipelagos. In 1857, London opened a consulate at Levuka, the ancient capital of Fiji and in 1874, after years of inconclusive and bloody tribal feuding, convinced King Cakobau to hand over power to the consul and allow him to establish order. A British base was founded in 1870 on the island of Guadalcanal (Solomon Islands) to import forced labor to the sugarcane plantations of Australia and Fiji and, in 1873, the entire archipelago became a British protectorate. After the establishment of British and French plantations on various islands, Vanuatu (then known as the New Hebrides) became a joint French and British colony. In 1872, the United States obtained a concession for the installation of a naval base at Pago Pago, Samoa, whilst Great Britain and Germany contested the Samoan islands of Upolu and Savaii lacerated by tribal conflicts. In 1884, Germany transformed its settlements on the north-east coast of New Guinea into a colony, whilst the British colonized the south-eastern regions. On the collapse of the Spanish colonial empire in 1885, Germany and the United States shared Micronesia, with Guam going to the Americans and the Germans adjudicating the Marianas, the Marshall and the Caroline Islands. In 1887, the king of Hawaii permitted the United States Navy to establish a base at Pearl Harbor. Thanks to a law passed in 1848, the majority of the land had become American property and therefore in 1893, Sanford Ballard Dole, the representative from Washington felt authorized to take power with a coup d'état backed by the marines. In

44 top Paul Gauguin arrived in Polynesia in 1891 in search of the original colors of the world. He painted and sculpted, inspired by the nudity of the Polynesian women, the warm Pacific light, the tropical nature and the magical elements of Maohi spirituality.

44 bottom The women of Tahiti were the principal inspiration for the canvases of Paul Gauguin who fell in love with an adolescent native. Audacious paintings such as "Tahitian Women", "Nativity" and "Barbarian Stories" revealed all the color, the potency and the immense sensuality of Polynesia.

R. L. STEVENSON.

1897, the Hawaiian Islands were formally annexed by the United States. The Cook Islands became a British protectorate in 1888, while Easter Island was acquired by Chile. In 1899, an agreement led to the partitioning of Samoa, the islands of Upolu and Savaii going to Germany, and that of Tutuila (Pago Pago) to the United States. The only archipelago to retain its independence was the Kingdom of Tonga, thanks to a centralized power structure that managed to withstand the impact of the western powers. Paradoxically, while the Pacific culture declined under the colonial yoke, the myth of the South Sea islands spread throughout the world, accompanied by the fable of beautiful women who lived naked and practiced free love. Sailors, enchanted by the eroticism of the Hawaiian *hula* and the Tahitian *tamure*, propagated the legend of the fabulously sensuous Polynesians. Shapely women with velvet skin, long jet-black hair, Oriental eyes, high cheekbones and full lips like those painted by Paul Gauguin who, on an island in the Marquesas archipelago, ended his days in the arms of an adolescent. Between the second half of the nineteenth and the beginning of the twentieth centuries, writers of the calibre of Herman Melville, Mark Twain, Somerset Maugham, Jack London, Pierre Loti and Robert Louis Stevenson arrived in Polynesia in search of the exotic. They set novels in Honolulu, Samoa, the Marquesas and Tahiti that perpetuate the literary legend of the Southern Seas.

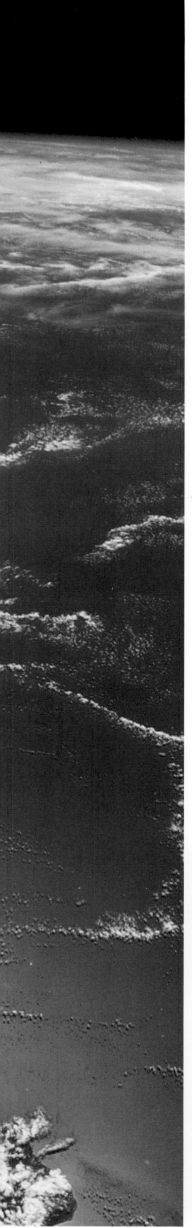

Polynesia means "many islands" and rather than a precise geographic entity the term describes the collection of islands, atolls and archipelagos colonized as a consequence of the Maori diaspora. A migratory movement that from "Nuclear Polynesia", roughly corresponding to the present-day states of Tonga and Samoa, scattered a seafaring population across a vast area of ocean. A cultural reality enclosed with an immense triangle whose extreme tips reach the Hawaiian archipelago, Easter Island and New Zealand. This enormous wedge of ocean contains 10,000 scraps of land covering a total of about 9,700 square miles (two thirds of which are accounted for by the Hawaiian Islands), that is to say about the same area as Sicily, while New Zealand, with the variety of its continental landscapes, covers an area slightly larger than that of Great Britain at 105,000 square miles. As a consequence of the European explorations and colonization, Polynesia has ceased to be an homogenous cultural entity for over a century. In all the archipelagos missionaries have converted the natives to Christianity. The new faith has radically changed the customs of the majority of islanders who, having lost their traditions, now lead increasingly westernised lifestyles. In the Hawaiian Islands, New Zealand and Easter Island the peoples of European origin now far outnumber the

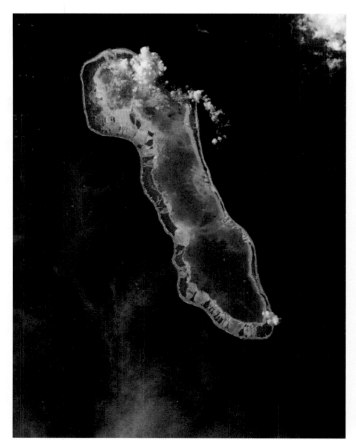

$\mathcal{P}$OLYNESIA: TEN THOUSAND ISLANDS FOR A SINGLE MYTH

Polynesian natives and have created modern western societies in which few traces of Polynesian culture remain. In French Polynesia, to which the Society Islands, the Tuamotu archipelago, the Gambier Islands, the Marquesas and the Austral Islands belong, the Maori heritage has been combined with European customs and Asiatic trade. Since the 1970s there has been a revival of Polynesian culture that in Tahiti, Hawaii and New Zealand has led to a rediscovery of dance, sculpture and tattooing. The Maori tradition has, instead, always been maintained in the Cook Islands and above all in Western Samoa and the Kingdom of Tonga, timeless archipelagos where the Polynesian myth lives on through dances, tattoos and relaxed rhythms.

The characters of Polynesia, Melanesia and

46-47 This photo, taken by a Nasa satellite, shows the range of volcanoes forming the Hawaiian archipelago (United States). From bottom left, diagonally, one can see the islands of Nihau, Kauai, Oahu, Molokai, Lanai, Maui, Kahoolawe and Hawaii.

47 top Another Nasa satellite photo showing Rangiroa atoll in the Tuamotu archipelago. Lagoon atolls are found in Micronesia and the Northern Group of the Cook Islands as well as in French Polynesia.

47 center An aerial photo of Rangiroa in the Tuamotu archipelago (French Polynesia) showing the structure of a motu, the strip of land—here no wider than 655 feet—formed on the emergent part of the coral reef enclosing the lagoon.

47 bottom The island of Hawaii was formed by the volcanoes Manua Loa, Manua Kea and Kilauea. This infra-red photo taken by Nasa reveals the differences between the forests (in dark red), the cultivated areas (pinkish), the volcanic peaks (grey-green) and recent lava flows (black).

48 In the Hawaiian archipelago, volcanoes emerged from the ocean depths via cracks in the earth's crust. Immense eruptions at depths of around 16,500 feet have spewed such quantities of magma as to create a range of mountains towering 13,000 feet above sea level. This photo shows the lava of the Kilauea volcano flowing into the water.

48-49 Kilauea is the last active volcano of the three that were responsible for the creation of the island of Hawaii. When they emerged from the ocean the islands composing the archipelago were sterile volcanic rocks on which life evolved over millions of years.

Islands, the Society Islands, the majority of the Hawaiian and Fijian islands, Rarotonga (Cook Islands), Tutuila (American Samoa) and Upolu (Western Samoa) that emerged ten million years ago and now feature time-eroded mountains and rocks blanketed with tropical rain forests. Some of these islands boast spectacular black sand beaches, the last stage in the process of orogenesis, fragments of volcanic rock rich in magnetite, olivine and pyroxenes. Other more recent islands such as Maui (Hawaii), Kao (Tonga), Savaii (Western Samoa), Lopevi (Vanuatu) and Tinakula (Solomon Islands) are still dominated by active volcanoes. This intense volcanic activity is due to the "Ring of Fire" surrounding the Pacific basin, the greatest chain of craters anywhere in the

An ocean of atolls and vulcanoes

Micronesia—the three regions into which the islands of the Pacific Ocean are divided—have more to do with their ethnic make-up than their improbable geological and morphological differences. Many of the archipelagos include atolls, low islands, emergent volcanic rocks, coral reefs and platforms of *makatea* - substrates of calcareous material of coralline origin. All of the Pacific islands are oceanic in nature; that is to say they have never been attached to a continent. The only exceptions to this rule are New Zealand, formed as a result of the south-east drift of Gondwanaland, and Papua New Guinea, which also derived from the fragmentation of the super-continent that linked Australia, Antarctica, India, Africa and South America. A host of islands rise from the Pacific plate, the expanse of the earth's crust forming the base of the northern and central areas of the ocean. The formation of various types of island is in one way or another associated with craters, eruptions and seismic activity. There are volcanic islands such as the Marquesas

world, within which occurs over four-fifths of all recorded telluric activity. The most intensive seismic ferment is concentrated in the Hawaiian region and the section of the Ring of Fire in which the Pacific plate is bordered by the Indo-Australian plate.

In the Hawaiian Islands during the middle Tertiary Period, volcanoes rose from the ocean depths via vertical cracks in the thin terrestrial crust. Immense eruptions at depths of around 16,500 feet threw out such quantities of magma as to create a mountain range peaking at over 13,000 feet above sea level. The Mauna Kea volcano on the island of Hawaii is, in fact the world's greatest mountain, rising almost 32,800 feet from the ocean floor (13,800 feet of which being above sea level) and thus topping Everest by almost 3,300 feet and exceeding the volume of Fuji in Japan a hundred-fold. Hawaii, also known as Big Island as with its 4,000 square miles it represents two thirds of all Hawaiian dry land, is the youngest island of the group. However, 15,500 miles to the south, at a depth of 3,300 feet, the genesis of the archipelago is still continuing; the Lo'ihi volcano is spewing magma a rate that means it will emerge above sea level within 9-10,000 years. At that point the story of life in the Pacific will begin again from zero. The seismic process is advancing towards the south-east because the Hawaiian Islands are situated on a mobile section of the Pacific plate drifting north-west at a rate of between 2 and 3 inches a year, whilst the submarine volcanic faults are stationary and continue to emit incandescent material.

Frenetic seismic activity is also recorded on New Zealand's North Island which is bisected by a chain of 150 volcanoes—some of which are still active—that snakes for over 200 miles between White Island in the Bay of Plenty and Mount Egmont. Its epicenter is in the Tongariro National Park, dominated by the three active volcanoes: Ruapehu, Tongariro and Ngauruhoe. Ruapehu—which in Maori means "exploding hole"—is the highest volcano on the island at 2,796 feet as well as one of the world's most turbulent. In the mid-nineties it produced dozens of violent eruptions, spectacular natural events with flowing lava, rocks being thrown into the air and ash clouds rising thousands of feet before falling in a radius of over 62 miles. This region to the north of the park is a boiling mosaic of craters, geysers, mud holes and sulphurous springs. Such intense volcanic activity is explained by New Zealand's geographical position: it rests on a segment of the Ring of Fire situated at the

49 top *The Pacific Ocean is surrounded by the Ring of Fire, the most extensive range of volcanoes to be found anywhere in the world. The greatest seismic activity is recorded in the Hawaiian region and in the section where Pacific and Indo-Australian plates collide.*

convergence of two tectonic plates. Here the thin Pacific plate slides under the denser Indo-Australian plate in a process known as subduction. The Pacific crust rests on the Benioff zone where it reaches melting temperature and the rocks liquefy, the magmatic material then emerging through fissures to form volcanoes. This geophysical process is still active and Rangitoto, an island in Auckland Bay, emerged above sea level only 800 years ago. The Melanesian archipelagos of New Caledonia, Vanuatu and the Solomon Islands are also situated on the fiery confine between the two plates. Subduction also occurs where the Pacific plate meets the continental Eurasian and North American plates. Oceanic abysses such as the Mariana Trench (Micronesia), part of which is known as the Challenger Deep, is the deepest point on earth at 36,200 feet, are opened at the plate margins as a consequence of

50 top The rocky nature of the 132 volcanic islands that composed the Hawaiian archipelago (the fiftieth American state) is revealed in this aerial photo. The Hawaiian archipelago is the only Polynesian island group to be located in the northern hemisphere. This photo shows a section of the coastline of Kauai.

50 bottom A classic holidaymaker's dream destination is a beach in the Hawaiian archipelago. Each year the islands welcome 7 million visitors while the rest of Polynesia, Melanesia and Micronesia combined receive less than a million tourists.

this process.

    Charles Darwin was the first man to study the geophysical phenomena of Oceania. During his five-year voyage (1831-1836) around the world aboard the *Beagle*, the British scientist formulated the theory whereby the atolls—sandy rings a few feet high surrounding salt-water lagoons—are the remains of eroded volcanoes. The rings are actually coral reefs that have emerged above the surface while the internal lagoons are the craters of sunken volcanoes. The madreporic material that surrounded their slopes has emerged as a result of the stratification of the fossilised polyps and have been covered with the white sand produced from the detritus of the coral reefs, fertilized by guano and sown with seeds carried by the sea. This is an on-going process in many of the Society Islands (French Polynesia) where strips of sand enclose lagoons overlooked by volcanoes as in the renowned Bora Bora and Huahine. Over millions of years erosion will transform these islands

50-51 An aerial photograph of Bora Bora (French Polynesia) confirming Darwin's theory whereby the atolls are formed by the sinking of the volcanoes and the motu by the emergence of coral reefs that have grown at their base. This phenomenon is still in progress on this island.

51 top The serpentine distribution of the seven islands composing the central backbone of the Ha'apai archipelago is seen in this aerial photo. In contrast with the other areas of the Kingdom of Tonga, these islands are completely flat and semi-arid with scarce vegetation and very little fresh water.

into flat atolls. With the *motu* (the islands composing the rings) dotted with coconut palms, the immaculate beaches and the lagoons rich in brilliantly colored fish, the atolls are one of the most enduring images of the primitive oceans. Atolls are found from the Polynesian Tuamotu and Cook Island to the Melanesian Fiji, Solomon Islands and New Caledonia and the Micronesian Marshall, Marianas, Caroline and Kiribati Islands.

In its turn the atoll, originating from a volcano, transforms into a *makatea* which in Maori means "white rock" and is the name of an island in the Tuamotu archipelago (French Polynesia) where the phenomenon of the stratification of coralline rocks was studied for the first time. Over tens of thousands of years this process leads the fossilized remains of the coral to transform the internal lagoons into calcareous plains, eliminating any link with the open sea. As a consequence, the salt-water lagoons become basins of fresh water, a phenomenon in progress in the case of Swains Island and Kiratimati in American Samoa. *Makatea* islands can also be found in Micronesia in the Palau, Marianas, Kiribati and Nauru archipelagos and in Polynesia in the Tonga, Samoa, Cook and Tuamotu groups. The distribution of the islands in the greatest of the oceans (the Pacific is the largest geographical entity on the planet with a surface area greater than that of all the dry land together) restricted the spread of flora and fauna.

On the arrival of the European explorers in eastern Polynesia (the Society Islands, the Marquesas, the Hawaiian Islands and the Cook Islands), only around fifteen plant species were found to be growing (coconut palms, screw-pines, breadfruit trees, ferns, hibiscus, gardenias, taro and other edible tubers). In Melanesia and western Polynesia (Tonga and Samoa), there were many more trees: banyans, strangling figs, flamboyance, acacias, mangroves, pines and melaleucas. The botanical profile of New Zealand was instead much richer thanks to the great environmental and climatic variety of the territory, with its extensive temperate rain forests allowing 2,700 plant species to be catalogued, the majority being endemic. In rainy New Guinea, where three-quarters of the territory is still covered with forests, pines, oaks and bamboo which grow on the plateaus and the mountain slopes at altitudes of between 3,300 and 11,500 feet, while the swamps contain hundreds of aquatic species and the river mouths are dominated by tangled mangroves. From the point of view of fauna, New Guinea is distinguished from the other Pacific archipelagos by the presence of wild pigs, an arboreal marsupial and almost a thousand different butterflies. From this point of view, New Zealand, despite its size and geographical complexity is not differentiated from the small oceanic islands. Mammals were originally limited to two species of giant bats and the seals that landed on the coasts of certain New Zealand and Hawaiian islands. During the ancient migrations from New Guinea and Southeast Asia, the ancestors of the Maoris introduced pigs, poultry, dogs and rats to many islands. Of the amphibians and reptiles there were just a few species of geckoes and frogs present on only a few islands; the only exception was the tuatara of New Zealand, a descendent (in miniature) of the dinosaurs whose evolution was completed 250 million years ago. Until the arrival of the Europeans, the Pacific was the undisputed kingdom of the birds to the extent that, given the absence of predators, many species lost the ability to fly and their wings atrophied. There are still numerous species of flightless birds, such as the cassowary of New Guinea, the kiwi of New Zealand (the symbol of the country) and a number of species of rallidae and parrots in various Polynesian archipelagos. The fate of the moa, the world's largest flightless bird—the giant species reached a height of almost 10 feet and weighed 530 pounds—was rather different: its very size made it a sought-after source of protein. In both New Zealand and Hawaii, the Maoris hunted the moa to extinction before the arrival of the Europeans, following it into the forests and flushing it out with fire. In the absence of reptiles, amphibians and predatory mammals, many plants also lost their natural defences which is why the Pacific region has few thorny species.

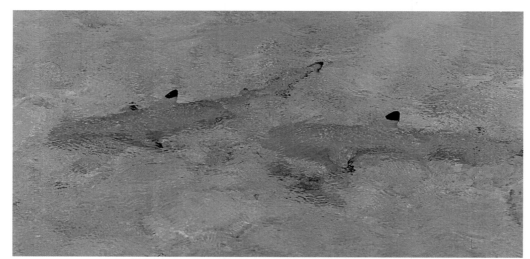

In contrast with those of the Melanesians, the physical and linguistic characteristics of the Polynesians were defined around 3,500 years ago, along the insular axis of New Caledonia, Fiji, Tonga and Samoa. According to some anthropologists, the cradle of Polynesian man was Tonga, where human presence is thought to date from 3000 BC, in spite of the fact that carbon 14 testing dates relics no earlier than 1100 BC. The history of Polynesia, enriched by legends and hypotheses, is full of uncertainties. On Tongatapu, black peoples from New Guinea mixed with various waves of immigrants from the Philippines, Indonesia, Vietnam and Southern China. This blend of Melanesians, Malays, Indonesians and Chinese is thought to have generated the Maoris, an ethnic group with sturdy bodies, amber skin, straight black hair, full lips and a distinctly Mongol appearance. There is more reliable information about the birth of Polynesia as a cultural entity as it coincides with the era of the Lapita people, the proto-Polynesian civilization that flourished between 1500 and 500 BC. Ceramists and navigators and empire builders, the Lapita people used the Tongatapu lagoon as a naval base and ranged among the islands of the present-day archipelagos of Samoa, Fiji and New Caledonia. Tonga was probably once the Lapita capital, a fact demonstrated according to a number of historians by the megalithic monuments and the pyramids discovered at

The Maori, vikings of the Pacific

54 top Sculpture represents the most important form of artistic expression for the Maoris. Sculpting is a divine activity learned from Tangaroa, the creator of the sea and the land. Statues of diverse forms can be found in almost all the Polynesian archipelagos. This picture shows a piece of sculpture from New Zealand's North Island.

54 bottom This sculpture can be found in the Maori Arts and Crafts Institute at Rotorua in New Zealand where the Maoris have sculpted with a vast range of materials including volcanic rock, wood, bone and jade as well as amber and shells used for inlaying wood.

Tongatapu, close to the ancient capital Mua. This hypothesis is supported by the successive constitution of a strong centralized power structure on Tonga, unique in the Pacific, a kingdom capable of extending its influence over much of the Lapita empire. The name Lapita derives from the place in New Caledonia where ceramics decorated with curvilinear or geometric stripes were discovered for the first time and allowed the still mysterious story of these peoples to be reconstructed. The decline of the Lapita people occurred around 500 BC, and was probably caused by a new migratory wave from New Guinea. What is certain is that black peoples invaded New Caledonia and much of Fiji. Whilst in New Caledonia, the Melanesian physical and linguistic characteristics prevailed, in Fiji they were mixed with those of the Polynesians. The Melanesian invasion that led to the decline of the Lapita is testified on a number of Polynesian islands within the Fijian archipelago: the Lau archipelago, for centuries claimed by Tonga, but also Rotuma in the north, a Maori microcosm in the middle of Melanesia. There is instead dwindling support for the hypothesis that the Polynesians arrived from South America, as Thor Heyerdahl attempted to demonstrate in 1947 with the famous voyage of the Kon-Tiki, a raft similar to those used by the Precolumbians with which the Norwegian archaeologist sailed from Peru to the Tuamotu archipelago.

With the confines and characteristics of "Nuclear" Polynesia established, we can see how these Stone Age people managed to colonize islands scattered across a vast area of ocean during the course of a millennium. At the root of the migratory process were the Polynesian social structure and the overcrowding of the islands. Society hinged on the extended family and was rigidly divided into classes. On most islands the population was divided into Ariki (tribal chieftains) and common people. In the Hawaiian archipelago, Tahiti and Tonga, a kind of land-owning aristocracy formed

54-55 The moai, the huge anthropomorphic statues from Easter Island, fascinated the early explorers, but their origin long remained a mystery capable of generating inventive hypotheses that involved extraterrestrials and an island cemetery for the whole of Polynesia.

55 The tiki, anthropomorphic statues in stone found in the saturated jungle of Hiva Oa and Nuku Hiva, two islands in the Polynesian Marquesas group, were sculpted between 1440 and 1700. They dominated the marae, ceremonial platforms on which human sacrifices were performed. The largest Nuku Hiva ceremonial center could hold up to 10,000 people.

an intermediate class, whilst on the Cook and Gambier Islands and in New Zealand there were slaves, above all enemies captured during tribal conflicts. The concept of private property was unknown throughout Polynesia, land being collectively owned by the clans. And, with the exception of Tonga, there was no central power, social order on the various islands being guaranteed by priests or the *Ariki* through *mana* (spiritual authority) associated with a variable series of taboos.

On the death of the *Ariki* the first-born son succeeded his father, whilst his brothers and their respective clans (dozens or even hundreds of individuals) took to sea in canoes in search of uninhabited land. This migratory pattern avoided a demographic explosion on islands with economies based on subsistence agriculture. Overpopulation was, in fact, behind such cruel practices as infanticide and cannibalism. This last was one of the common features of the various Pacific archipelagos, being found from Fiji to the Marquesas and New Zealand. On most islands it was above all a ritual custom, with enemies killed in battle being eaten to acquire their *mana* or spiritual power. In the crowded Marquesas Islands instead, any individual who violated the taboos regulating life in the archipelago was eaten. Here the need to maintain order was combined with the need to exploit all possible food resources in an ungenerous land. The legendary Hawaiki, supposedly the source of the Polynesian diaspora, is identified by most experts as the Samoan island of Savaii. The order and time-scale whereby the archipelagos were colonized are still the object of debate amongst the historians and archaeologists. The most reliable hypothesis is that around 300 BC, the Samoans undertook the migration that, in the early years of the modern era, took them to the Marquesas and a number of the Society Islands; probably to Raiatea and Huahine, the islands that conserve the most archaeological relics. The most important of these remains are the *marae*, the stone platforms on which religious ceremonies were celebrated. What is certain is that Raiatea had an important cultural role: governed by the *Aroi*, a group with astronomical and mediumistic knowledge, it was for centuries the spiritual and intellectual center of Polynesia. Here, James Cook encountered a priest with cartographic knowledge that included the Society Islands, Samoa, the

Marquesas and the Cook Islands. Elements that have induced some, such as the American writer James Michener, to claim that Raiatea should be recognized as the legendary Hawaiki, the cradle of Polynesia. Between 400 and 500 AD, the Maoris spread from the Marquesas islands to Hawaii, the Tuamotu archipelago and Easter Island. In the tenth century, probably departing from the Society Islands, they reached the Cook Islands and then New Zealand, where from the 13th century they developed an aggressive farming civilization. The history of the peopling of the Pacific reveals the extraordinary seafaring skills of the Maoris. With canoes around 65 feet long and equipped with a pair of sails, they tackled the greatest of the oceans, exploiting its winds and currents. They navigated using the night skies as nautical charts, intuiting the nearby presence of islands by the direction of the waves, and marking the seas they had already explored on empirical maps of woven bamboo. There are those who attribute the physical bulk of the Maoris, the world's largest people, to the extremely severe process of natural selection that took place during their interminable ocean voyages.

Even though many archipelagos remained isolated for centuries, the Maoris from Hawaii to New Zealand through to Samoa speak similar languages, have similar physical characteristics and, despite their universal conversion to Christianity, all refer to the same religious roots. Their faith was based on divinities in whom a human appearance was combined with an accentuated spiritual power. At the origin of the Maori universe lay Tangaroa, the god of the sea, creation and fertility, and guardian of the art of sculpture. The divine activity par excellence, sculpture, is the most widespread Maori art. In various forms it is present in almost all the archipelagos: from the stone *tiki* (the anthropomorphic statues) that dominate the *marae* buried in the damp jungles of the Marquesas to the *moai*, the giant busts of Easter Island, from the images of Tangaroa equipped with a gigantic phallus carved into the trunks of coconut palms on the Cook Islands to the jade idols of New Zealand and the grotesque divinities with mother-of-pearl eyes and coconut fibre hair of the Hawaiian Islands. The Maoris have worked any material they

56 left This photo illustrates one of the traditional dances performed in the Marquesas Islands (French Polynesia) where dances are accompanied by chanting and drums.

56 center The most common of the Tahitian dances is the tamure, *a sensual rhythm performed by the women only and very similar to the Hawaiian hula. Other dances in which the men also participate, such as the one depicted in this photograph, refer to ancient rituals of war.*

56 right The tamure, *considered to be a sinful dance, was prohibited by the European missionaries in the second half of the nineteenth century. It was revived in the 1950s and 1960s, initially as part of the islanders' search for their cultural roots and later as an exotic art capable of stimulating tourism.*

57 The first explorers were responsible for spreading the myth of the Polynesian women who lived naked and were inclined to free love. Shapely girls with velvet skin, long black hair, Oriental eyes, high cheekbones and full lips.

58-59 This photo shows a Polynesian fisherman with a harpoon in one of the Cook Islands lagoons. In this archipelago, situated to the west of Tahiti, the inhabitants use all kinds of fishing techniques, rods, drag nets and even a kind of machete with which they spear the fish in shallow waters.

58 bottom The inhabitants of Bora Bora entertain visitors with shark feeding trips. The innocuous small sharks of the lagoon are fed with scraps of fresh tuna whilst the tourists equipped with masks and attached to a pole observe the show from beneath the surface.

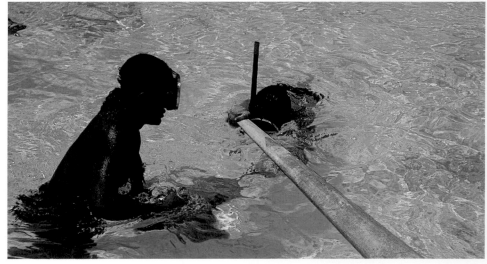

have found in their various adopted homelands, from volcanic rock to tropical hardwood, from bone to jade, amber and shells used for inlays in wood. Having no form of writing with the exception of the *rongo rongo*, the hieroglyphs of Easter Island, they at times used sculpture to record their history. The carvings on the beams in the meeting houses of New Zealand are actually family trees, a series of figured names and events through which the Maoris are able to reconstruct the stories of their tribes. In New Zealand where, thanks to the immense interior, the Maoris enjoyed their greatest demographic expansion and having abandoned the art of navigation developed a warrior culture, sculpture took the form of bellicose weapons and symbols. These ranged from the decoration of spears and maces to frightening ornaments on the prows of the canoes with the tattooed face of a man with a protruding tongue. This last image synthesises the three most important forms of expression in Polynesia combining sculpture with tattooing and the protruding tongue that evokes the *haka*, the Maori war dance.

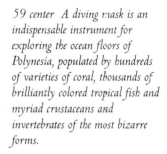

Apart from New Zealand, where this aggressive aspect prevailed in all forms of art, throughout Polynesia dance took on above all sensual overtones. The Tahitian *tamure* is akin to the Hawaiian *hula* and the dances of Tonga, the Cook Islands and the Marquesas, in the frenetic movement with which the Polynesian women rotate their behinds while keeping their torsos still. What to us appears to be an erotic art was according to Hawaiian mythology invented on Molokai, the island of moon goddess, as a sacred ritual dedicated to the gods of the sky. The *haka heva* of the Marquesas islands instead had explicit sexual references with the most beautiful girls of the village dancing naked around the dead in an attempt to revive them by playing on sexual instincts. Like dance, tattooing was also practiced in much of Polynesia and became a fundamental element in the culture of New Zealand and the Marquesas where men and women decorated much of the bodies. It was a rite of initiation practiced from puberty onwards, using extremely painful techniques. The motivations for the tattooing were different according to sex, status and clan: the Maoris considered tattoos to be talismans capable of protecting them from disease and giving them courage in battle.

59 top This photo shows a Maori with his body covered with tattoos, a widespread custom for thousands of years in much of Polynesia where ritual motifs were incised on the skin from puberty onwards. Depending on the motifs used, the tattoos recorded the sex, age, clan or status of the person.

59 center A diving mask is an indispensable instrument for exploring the ocean floors of Polynesia, populated by hundreds of varieties of coral, thousands of brilliantly colored tropical fish and myriad crustaceans and invertebrates of the most bizarre forms.

59 bottom This Polynesian fisherman is instead fishing underwater, a very common and highly efficient technique in the lagoons of the coral atolls which are frequently inhabited by hundreds of species of fish. In some lagoons such as those of Rangiroa and Manihi, night dives are also made.

60-61 *A Maori celebration on Waitangi Day, the national festival of New Zealand and the anniversary of the signing of the treaty whereby the tribal chieftains conceded sovereignty of the two islands to the British crown in return for land rights.*

60 bottom *On the occasion of Waitangi Day, on February 6, in the waters of the Bay of Islands, a race between war canoes is staged. The Maoris were great navigators, capable of traversing the Pacific Ocean in frail canoes using the night sky as a nautical chart.*

61 top This young Maori is wearing a costume introduced in the early twentieth century to cover the nudity of the Maori dancers. Around her waist she is wearing the poi, linen balls tied to cords and used, in the new forms of dance, as a female choreographic instrument.

61 bottom A Maori warrior engaged in the celebrated Haka war dance. The photo highlights a number of characteristic elements of the Haka dance such as the protruding tongue and the symbol of maximum aggression, the raised club ready to strike. The painted face features ritual motifs with which the Maori of New Zealand once tattooed their entire bodies. The bellicose traditions of the Maoris and the notable aggression they demonstrated obliged the English to negotiate agreements with the natives during the period in which New Zealand was colonized.

62 top *The landscape of the Southern Alps, a mountain range of relatively recent formation (around 10 million years ago) with permanent glaciers and 27 peaks of almost 10,000 feet in height which runs along much of the western side of New Zealand's South Island. This photo shows one of the peaks in the mountain range, Mount Ngauruhoe.*

62-63 *At 9,171 feet, Mount Ruapehu is the highest peak of New Zealand's North Island. Situated in the Tongariro National Park, it is an active volcano whose last eruption between 1995 and 1997 produced lava flows, launched rocks high into the air and created vast clouds of ashes.*

New Zealand:

63 top The Rotorua region on North Island is New Zealand's largest area of thermal activity thanks to an infinite number of geysers, hot springs, mud baths and sulphureous waters. These elements have encouraged the development of the greatest density of Maori communities in the country. The vapors seen here are given off by the Te-Whakarewakarewa Pohutu geyser.

63 bottom The volcano of White Island in the Bay of Plenty has a perennial plume of smoke. The bay is the starting point of a range of 150 volcanoes, some of which are still active, snaking for about 125 miles across North Island as far as Mount Egmont.

a corner of Europe in the southern seas

The Kiwis, the name given to the New Zealanders in reference to the flightless bird that has become the national symbol, are stubborn people; the heirs of British seal hunters who landed on South Island in 1792, they have always lived in symbiosis with nature. Today the adventurers have given way to the environmentalists and New Zealand is the cleanest and most closely protected country in the world. The Anglo-Saxon love of nature is combined with an open-air lifestyle. The Kiwis love trekking, climbing and sailing; sports they practice among the mountains, lakes, bays and spectacular landscapes that created by the orogenesis of the western Pacific rim. Composed of two islands situated between the 34th and 47th parallels south on a longitudinal axis stretching 995 miles, New Zealand is the emergent part of the ocean that surrounds it, with its corrugated crests and valleys formed as a result of submarine seismic activity. Resting on the Ring of Fire, the country is traversed by mountain ranges of recent formation: the Southern Alps of South Island decline towards North Island in an arc of active and extinct volcanoes. Although they were united in the Ice Age, the two islands are geologically and morphologically distinct. The interior of South Island with its forests, glaciers, peaks and lakes is reminiscent of the European Alps, especially Mount Cook, the country's highest summit at 12,346 feet. Mount Cook rises in a national park that contains 22 of New Zealand's 27 mountains of over 9,800 feet in height. Its rock walls are the most famous mountaineering terrain in Oceania and were the training ground for Sir Edmund Hillary, the New Zealander who in 1953 became the first man to conquer Everest. A curious landscape mirage can be seen on the West Coast, locked in by the glaciers and the fury of the Tasman Sea which is swept by the Roaring Forties, the prevailing winds of the lower latitudes. Tongues of snow snake between the arboreal ferns of the temperate rain forest a few miles from the coast. Further south in Fiordland, successive ice ages created dozens of fjords, their slopes covered with luxuriant vegetation thanks to a climate that drenches the region with an average annual rainfall of 275 inches. Here, over the last 500 million years, the forces of erosion have sculpted breathtaking landscapes, a succession of inlets, bays, rock walls, snow-fields, lakes, streams and waterfalls, home to penguins, albatross, seals,

dolphins and parrots. Just a few hours' drive away, however, is the modern face of Fiordland, Queenstown, situated on Lake Wakatipu, the world capital of extreme sports from heli-skiing to white-water rafting and canoeing, from skydiving to scree-slope skiing, from hangliding to bungee jumping. This last sport, now practiced throughout the world, was invented here in 1986 by the downhill skier Henry van Ash, and was based on an initiation ritual from Vanuatu. Christchurch, South Island's largest city, instead represents the island's most conventional face, if that is the right way to describe an apparently English city with certain Kiwi quirks, such as being able to reach the center by kayak on the River Avon. In sharp contrast with the urban center of what is the least populated island (housing a quarter of the total New Zealand population of 3,600,000 people), is Kaikoura where one can enjoy close encounters with sperm and humpback whales migrating from Antarctica for the mating season.

North Island is instead characterized by a belt of active volcanoes bisecting the island. The northernmost region is sub-tropical with damp forests, long beaches and bays studded with islands, sailing paradises such as the Bay of Islands and Hauraki Gulf. While South Island represents the uncontaminated aspect of the country, North Island embodies its history and culture, housing Wellington and Auckland, respectively the largest city and the capital. The island is heavy with Maori tradition and myths, the ethnic

group composing 13% of the population, many living between Hawke Bay and Auckland with their spiritual center at Rotorua, the location of the school of the divine art of sculpture. North Island also highlights the extremely civilized side of New Zealand, a pioneer in terms of social justice and the emancipation of women who were granted the vote as early as 1893. The British immigrants in New Zealand were the aristocrats of colonialism who moved to the Antipodes to establish immense farms. When London granted them self-government in 1852, the future of the country was already oriented towards large-scale animal husbandry and with the invention of refrigerated ships, New Zealand became a key supplier of meat to the United Kingdom. This development allowed Wellington to actuate revolutionary social reforms and the country's inhabitants to enjoy a high standard of living as it became the cradle of the welfare state. In 1898 it became the first country to introduce old age pensions and protected the weakest social classes with subsidies, guaranteed medical care and free education. It was Britain's entrance into the European Common Market in 1973 that changed this situation as the British were obliged to purchase European rather New Zealand goods and the Kiwis had to reinvent their economy. They turned to Japan, the United States and the developing countries of Asia and, after a long period of recession, reformed the state welfare system. The standard of living in New Zealand remains, however, one of the highest in the world with four-fifths of the inhabitants living in their own homes and enjoying good education and a healthy, open-air lifestyle. This last element is fundamental and is combined with a passion for sport. Competitive activities are widely practiced in all age groups and social strata, favored by public facilities for rugby, cricket, tennis and golf. 1,400,000 New Zealanders are members of 150 sporting clubs. Sailors by instinct and tradition, the Kiwis also boast the greatest density of boats in the world and win many of the international sailing prizes. Their love of the sea is combined with that for adventure, reflecting the audacity of a population of pioneers who have always measured themselves against nature and the tyranny of distance that confined western peoples in the Southern Seas. The sense of isolation felt by the New Zealanders is graphically illustrated by an episode that took place some years ago. An Air New Zealand plane crashed in Antarctica, and the passengers were killed. A period of national mourning was declared but there was also a sense of pride because for the first time New Zealand had appeared on the front pages of newspapers throughout the world.

64 top The west coast of South Island is in part covered with patches of temperate rain-forest with ferns and rare plants such as the white pine (Podocarpus dacrydiodes), New Zealand's tallest tree. The entire region is protected by UNESCO.

64-65 The small town of Glenorchy, situated on Lake Wakatiou on New Zealand's South Island, is surrounded by the magnificent scenery of the Remarkables, a mountain range boasting a number of very popular winter skiing resorts.

64 bottom The Coromandel peninsula in the North Island , composed of hills and mountains incised with tumbling streams and largely covered with rain-forests, extends for over 620 miles on the east side of Hauraki Gulf, opposite the city of Auckland.

65 bottom Lake Tekapo is situated in the southern region of Canterbury (South Island) on a plateau of the eastern slopes of Mount Cook. On the shores of the lake stands the village of the same name which is frequented by climbers during the summer and skiers in the winter.

66-67 The city of Queenstown is the New Zealand capital of winter and extreme sports and the country's most popular tourist destination. It is situated at an altutude of 1,017 feet in a magnificent setting between Lake Wakatipu and the snow-covered peaks of the Remarkables.

66 bottom left Wellington, the capital of New Zealand, is situated in the hills that surround the Lambton Bay. It is an extremely green city with parks on the sea front and around the business district characterized by a cluster of skyscrapers that overshadow the Parliament building.

66 bottom right This aerial photo shows Rotorua, a city with 60,000 inhabitants (including a large Maori community) situated in the heart of North Island. The city stands at the center of a region composed of fourteen lakes and surrounded by forests and hills grazed by livestock.

67 top Christchurch is the largest—with no less than 330,000 inhabitants—and most important city of New Zealand's South Island, and is situated in the center of the Canterbury region. This photo shows Cathedral Square, the city's social hub and a meeting place for young people. It is occasionally enlivened by the presence of bizarre preachers.

67 bottom Auckland is the principal city of New Zealand with a population of a million people and extends for almost 50 miles along a north-south axis. The inhabited area overlooks Hauraki Gulf, a bay dotted with forty-seven islands that is considered to be one of the best venues in the world for competitive sailing.

68-69 Mount Cook, 3,765 feet (12,350 feet), is New Zealand's highest mountain. It is situated at the center of the national park of the same name that extends over a surface area of 270 square miles and includes 22 of the 27 mountains of the Southern Alps reaching over 9,800 feet in height.

68 bottom Mount Cook is New Zealand's greatest climbing venue. Sir Edmund Hillary, the New Zealander who in 1953 became the first man to reach the summit of Mount Everest, made his first climb here at 16 years of age in 1935.

69 top New Zealand is considered to be a paradise for treking enthusiasts, thanks to a complex network of footpaths that lead walkers through rain-forests, national parks and mountains and frequently snake along spectacular stretches of coastline.

69 bottom This photo of the glacier on Mount Ruapehu, 2,796 feet (9,171 feet), shows that New Zealand's highest and most turbulent volcano is also an important ski resort. The center of activities and winter sports is the village of Ohakune.

70 top *Rugby union is New Zealand's most popular sport with a million players actively involved. The country's pride and joy is the powerful All Blacks team featuring Maoris from both of the country's principal islands as well as from various Polynesian archipelagos.*

70 center left *A group of people involved in a game of bowls. This sport is widely played in New Zealand and matches are very much a social occasion with the players obliged to follow precise rules and an all-white dress code.*

70 center right *The powerful Shotover torrent in the Queenstown region (South Island) is the venue for various extreme sports. It is navigated by flat-bottomed power boats capable of reaching 75 kph as well as by the inflatable rafts (seen in the photo).*

70 bottom *The New Zealanders are the world's greatest sailing skippers. After having won the Whitbread race, Peter Blake broke every record in the book by sailing round the world in 75 days. Sailing is so popular in New Zealand that in Auckland there are 70,000 boats for a population of less than 1,000,000.*

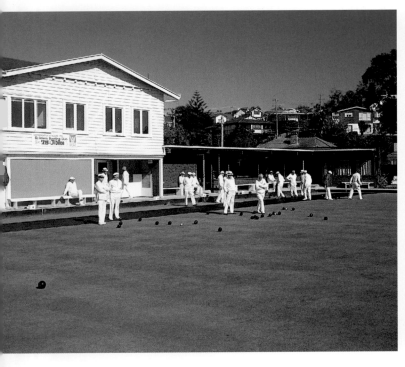

71 *A kayak braves the Gates of Argonaut, a spectacular gorge on the River Hokitika on the west coast of South Island. The New Zealanders combine their love of nature with a passion for sport. They are dynamic people accustomed to spending a lot of time in the open air and to braving the elements. A typical* Kiwi holiday includes long treks through the temperate rain-forests or along the paths that in a number of national parks follow the shoreline. Canoes, kayaks and rafts are used to explore rivers and internal lakes, while sailing boats are the most popular means of travelling along the coasts.

72-73 This photo of Moorea (French Polynesia) shows Cook Bay, one of the two large inlets that open on the north coast of a garden island dominated by six steeply descending volcanic peaks with valleys in which pineapples and vanilla are cultivated.

Polynesia:

73 top Beaches of white sand and magnificent landscapes are waiting to be discovered within the lagoons, but tourism in French Polynesia is nonetheless restricted to around a dozen islands, meanwhile hundreds of paradisical slivers of land lack any form of infrastructure for receiving visitors.

73 center The beaches of Polynesia are frequently deserted because, in spite of the beauty of the landscapes, the number of visitors is severely restricted by the enormous distances from Europe and the United States, the principal sources of international tourism.

the islands painted by Gauguin

With palm-fringed rings of sand framing the lagoons, volcanoes cloaked in jungle vegetation that redden in the sunset and tattooed natives riding through dripping forests, French Polynesia offers the most convincing postcard images of Oceania. The group in which Tahiti is the principal island is composed of five archipelagos accounting for a total of 1,521 square miles of dry land scattered across an area of ocean half the size of Europe. The Society Islands, where Tahiti, Bora Bora and many of the locations that have contributed to the Polynesian myth are to be found, are in turn divided into two clusters known as the Leeward and the Windward Islands. The name "Society Islands" was originally given to the Leeward Islands by James Cook because they were closely grouped. Later the definition was extended to the Windward Islands, Tahiti, Moorea, Tetiaroa, Maiao and Mehetia. All the islands are volcanic in origin, with the exception of the atoll Tetiaroa. The highest peak is on Tahiti, but the most dramatic landscape is provided by Moorea, with volcanic cones descending in rugged valleys towards vanilla and pineapple plantations and the deep Cook and Hopunohu Bays. The peaks stand in sharp contrast with the lagoon enclosed within coral reefs and beaches rimmed with palms. The landscape of Bora Bora, the most beautiful of the Leeward islands, is also impressive with its twin volcanoes reflected in the turquoise waters of a lagoon populated by 200 species of fish and enclosed by a belt of motus, the tongues of sand that form on the coral reefs. The natural scenery of Bora Bora has on a number of occasions been exploited by the motion picture industry which has transformed the island into a celebrated destination for the international jet set. In recent years, however, its fame has in part been eclipsed by Huahine, an island that combines fabulous landscapes with important archaeological remains. Excavations have brought to light 94 marae, the traditional spiritual meeting places, from the 16th century, and a village from 650 AD, buried by a mysterious cataclysm, a kind of Polynesian Pompeii with objects and tools still lying in the houses. A club has been found with decorative motifs similar to those used by the Maori of New Zealand. This find lends support to the theory of those who attribute the role of Hawaiki, the island from which the original Maori diaspora departed, to Raiatea (the religious and political fulcrum of Polynesia) rather than the Samaoan Savaii as suggested by the majority of Oceanic historians.

To the north-east of Tahiti lies the Tuamotu archipelago,

73 bottom Polynesia, described by the early European explorers as the Garden of Eden, originally had only around fifteen botanical species. The plants introduced by the Maori migrations and by the western colonies have increased the number of species present to around 120. The Polynesian flora is a compound reality with significant differences between the eastern and western archipelagos.

composed of 78 atolls. Here can be found paradisical islands such as Rangiroa, Manihi, Fakarava and Tikehau, rings of white sand, dotted with palms, enclosing blue lagoons teaming with brilliantly colored fish. There are destinations for diving enthusiasts but also sites for the cultivation of black pearls. The name of the Tuamotu islands is sadly associated with the French nuclear testing; between 1966 and 1995 the eastern islands of Moruroa and Fangataufa have witnessed the explosion of 181 atomic or hydrogen bombs. To the east of these radioactive atolls is the Gambier archipelago, ten rocky islands enclosed within a single coral reef. To the north rise the imposing volcanic platforms of the Marquesas group, ten islands sweating in a torrid equatorial climate with mountainous interiors cloaked with jungle vegetation, criss-crossed by rough tracks and studded with *tiki*, anthropomorphic sculptures than dominate the ceremonial platforms. A land as harsh as it is intriguing, a destination for *recherche sauvage*, it is no coincidence that restless spirits such as the Belgian singer-songwriter Jacques Brel and the French painter Paul Gauguin ended there days here. The Marquesas Islands were peopled in the early years of the Christian era, and a few centuries later Maori navigators set sail from here to colonize the Hawaiian Islands, Easter Island, the Tuamotu archipelago, the Gambier Islands and a number of the Society Islands. To the south of Tahiti can instead be found the isolated Austral group composed of five volcanic islands.

The arrival of the Europeans in the late eighteenth century rocked the mainstays of the rigid class system on which Polynesian society had been based. The attempt made by the Pomare dynasty to unite a number of islands in a single kingdom was unable to deflect the expansionist aims of the colonists. The French claim on Tahiti made by Bougainville in 1768 was not followed up, but the weakening of the Tahitian monarchy—a result of the drastic demographic fall caused by diseases imported by the European sailors and the mass conversion to Christianity—reawakened French ambitions. Following the imposition of a consul in 1838, a French

stratagem succeeded in transforming the Windward Islands into a French protectorate in 1842. In 1887, the British-controlled Leeward Islands passed to France which, one-by-one, invaded all the other archipelagos and, in 1900, declared the entire region to be a French colony. Despite the existence of an independence movement, in a 1958 referendum the majority of the population approved the archipelagos' ties with Paris. The installation of military bases followed, as did the development of the tourist industry, innovations that radically changed the islands. French Polynesia now boasts the highest standard of living and the best infrastructure in the region, but the free spirit of a population of navigators has been exchanged for the promise of a job in a public sector employing half of the islands' workers. The pure Maohi represent less than a fifth of the total population of 230,000, while Papeete, the chaotic capital, is increasingly similar to a western city, with traffic polluting the myth of the world's most exotic islands.

74 top A man leading horses along the beach of Taiohae, the capital of Nuku Hiva. Horses, today a symbol of the Marquesas Islands, were introduced to the archipelago by the Europeans. They are used intensively in the interior where they provide a means of transport over even the most difficult of terrain.

74 center Hatiheu Bay on the north-west coast of Nuku Hiva is dominated by a spectacular diadem of rocky pinnacles that rise in brilliantly green valleys full of millions of coconut palms. Nuku Hiva is the administrative center and largest island in the Marquesas archipelago.

74 bottom The emporium in which Paul Gauguin purchased absinthe can be seen in this photo of Atuona, the principal village on Hiva Oa. The painter settled on the island in 1894, painted a number of his most famous canvases and died here on the 27th of March, 1903. His tomb can be seen in the Atuona cemetery.

75 The north coast of Hiva Oa offers breathtaking scenery with towering peaks cloaked in tropical vegetation and spectacular bays. This is the second largest island in the Marquesas archipelago and between 1904 and 1944 was also the administrative center.

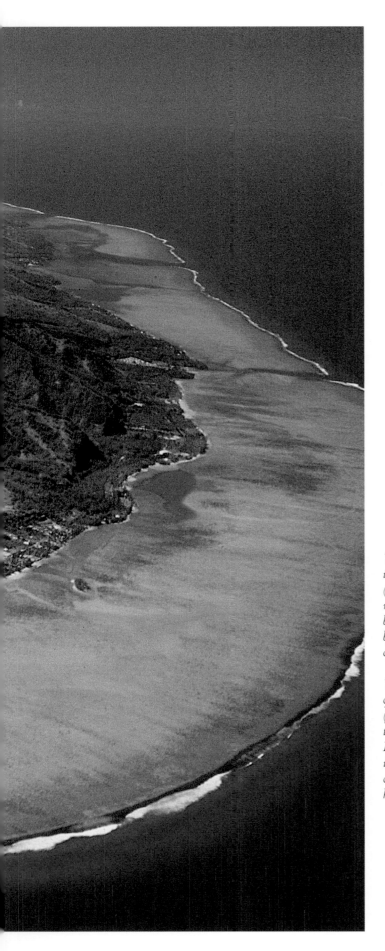

76-77 An aerial photo of Moorea in the Society Islands archipelago (French Polynesia). In the center rise steep volcanic peaks surrounded by a turquoise lagoon, itself enclosed by a coral reef protecting it from the open sea.

76 bottom This photo shows one of the two steep volcanoes (frequently enveloped in clouds) that dominate the island of Bora Bora and the surrounding lagoon, in the transparent waters of which over two hundred species of fish have been recorded.

77 top This photo portraying a group of palms on the island of Bora Bora in the Society Islands (French Polynesia) exalts the extraordinary colors of the atoll: from the incredible blue of the lagoon, considered to be one of the most spectacular in the world, thanks to a number of paradisical islets such as Motu Tapu, to the emerald green of the dense vegetation and the brilliant white of the extremely fine sands.

77 center In this image the photographer has captured the clouds that, at sunset, are reflected in the lagoon of Bora Bora. Seen from the sky, this remarkable island seems to be a dazzling mirage of colors: the green of the vegetation, the black of the volcanic lava and the turquoise of the lagoon, brilliant tones set in the immense midnight-blue expanse of the Pacific Ocean.

77 bottom On Polynesian shorelines the vegetation reaches the very edge of the water. On these islands many plants frequently sink their roots into the shallow waters of the lagoons and many oceanic beaches are stabilized by the complex ramifications of mangroves.

78 top This aerial photo shows the Tetiaroa atoll situated in the Society Islands archipelago (French Polynesia), 26 miles to the north of Tahiti. This private island, owned by Marlon Brando, is composed of thirteen uninhabited motu covered with coconut palms.

78 center This coral reef encloses a lagoon containing a number of atolls. All of the Polynesian islands with the exception of the wild Marquesas group, are surrounded by reefs, incredibly complex marine ecosystems containing hundreds of species of fish.

78-79 A channel separates two Polynesian islands. The presence of coral reefs around the dry land, as can be seen on the right of the photo, created considerable navigational problems for the first European explorers of the region. These gaps allow the tidal flow to bring fresh water rich in nutrients from open sea to the interior of the lagoon, thus favoring the proliferation of submarine life.

78 bottom One of the motu composing the Tetiaroa atoll boasts a landing strip. The island is a marine and ornithological reserve surrounded by 34 miles of coral and houses a luxury resort run by the Polynesian former wife of Marlon Brando.

*79 bottom Tahiti, the largest
island and administrative capital of
French Polynesia is surrounded by a
coral reef. The coastlines of the
island are inhabited by a population
of 160,000 while the precipitous
interior is dominated by Mount
Orohéna (7,350 feet).*

80-81 *An aerial photo showing a number of the* motu *surrounding the Bora Bora lagoon. This is the most famous island in French Polynesia and has been used as the setting for many films, from the two editions of "Mutiny of the Bounty" to the blockbuster produced by Dino de Laurentis, "Hurricane".*

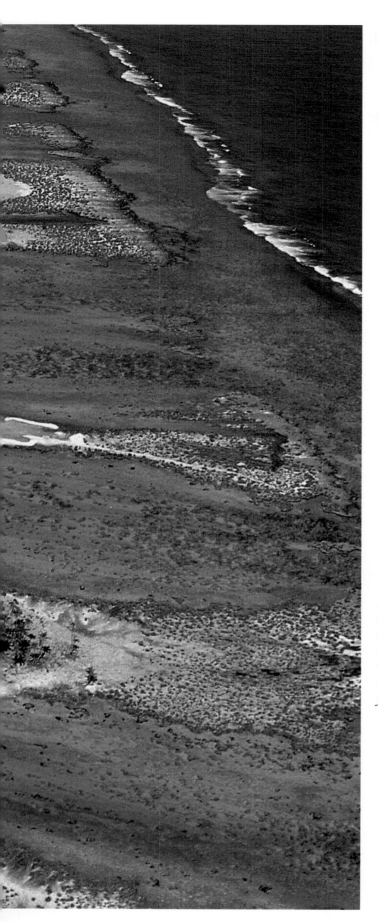

80 bottom Rangiroa atoll in the Tuamotu archipelego (French Polynesia) is composed of a strip of land about 143 miles long that encloses a lagoon with a surface area of 395 square miles within which a number of islets rise. Rangiroa is very popular with divers attracted by the extraordinary submarine fauna in its waters.

81 top A typical Polynesian outrigger canoe sailing in the Bora Bora lagoon, overlooked by the cores of two extinct volcanoes. The chromatic contrasts between the blue water, the green of the vegetation and the black of the rock have transformed the island into a landscape legend.

81 center This tongue of land is one of the motu composing Rangiroa. The emergent strips are at most 656 feet wide. The longest (6 miles) is Avatoru which has a population of 1,500 and boasts a school, two churches, an emporium, a hospital and a marine research station.

81 bottom This spectacular aerial view shows the long handle-like shape traced by the Tetiaroa atoll. Located off Tahiti, this is the only atoll in the Society Islands group which is otherwise composed of mountainous platforms of volcanic origins.

82 top left This young Polynesian is practicing fishing. In the shallow waters of some of the Polynesian lagoons, fish are caught with sharp spears. In contrast with what one might imagine, the primary source of food for the Polynesians was agriculture.

82 top right Islanders cultivate pearl oysters (Pinctada margaritifera) in the lagoons of some of the Tuamotu atolls. The islands of Manihi and Marutea are famous for the production of black pearls which are much more precious than the white variety and are mainly exported to Japan.

82-83 The incredible turquoise tones of the lagoon surrounding Bora Bora, the most famous Polynesian island, attracts stars such as Raquel Welch, Jane Fonda, Roman Polanski, Harrison Ford, Ringo Starr and Julio Iglesias.

82 bottom left A fish farm within the lagoon of one of the French Polynesian islands where the technique was introduced by the Europeans, partly because the traditional Polynesian economy was based on agriculture rather than fishing.

82 bottom right A Polynesian boy aboard a boat in the Rangiroa lagoon. French Polynesia was one of the great Pacific racial melting pots: the original Maohi population has mixed with Europeans, Americans and Asians.

83 top Coconuts have for centuries been the Polynesians' principal source of food and raw materials as they eat the meat, drink the milk, use the shells to make masks and decorations, the trunks of the palms to build huts and the fronds to make roofs.

83 center Coconut palm fronds are still used on many Polynesian islands for diverse purposes. They are useful in the construction of roofs and when woven serve to make tents, bags, head-dresses and traditional costumes.

83 bottom A Polynesian village on an atoll with the huts still built using palm trunks and fronds. Today the majority of the inhabitants of French Polynesia live in western-style wooden houses.

84 top *This aerial photo shows one of the Hawaiian Islands, an archipelago composed of six larger islands and a further 126 fragments of land. According to the Hawaiian creation myth, the archipelago was modelled by the goddess Pele together with her maids. In this photo, white clouds open to provide a glimpse of the fertile island of Hawaii, the largest in the archipelago.*

84-85 *Traces of the Menehune, a mysterious pre-Polynesian people, have been found on the Hawaiian island of Kauai seen here. The only reliable information we have about these people concerns their small stature, but they are the object of much speculation, particularly in regards to their ability to dam rivers.*

Hawaii Islands:

Polynesian stars and strips

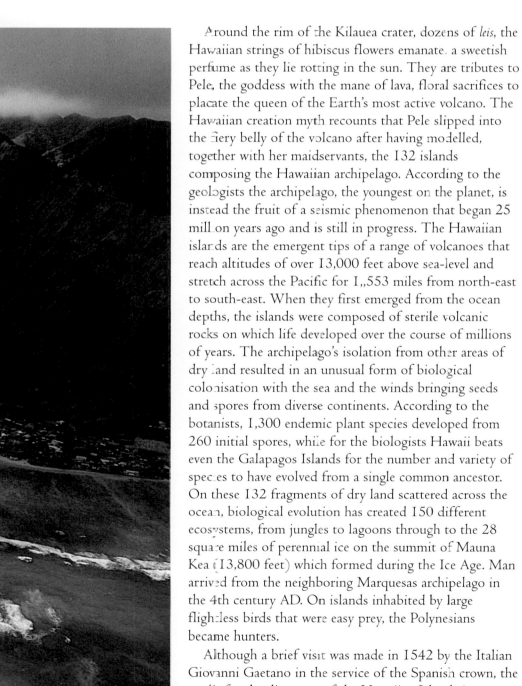

Around the rim of the Kilauea crater, dozens of *leis*, the Hawaiian strings of hibiscus flowers emanate a sweetish perfume as they lie rotting in the sun. They are tributes to Pele, the goddess with the mane of lava, floral sacrifices to placate the queen of the Earth's most active volcano. The Hawaiian creation myth recounts that Pele slipped into the fiery belly of the volcano after having modelled, together with her maidservants, the 132 islands composing the Hawaiian archipelago. According to the geologists the archipelago, the youngest on the planet, is instead the fruit of a seismic phenomenon that began 25 million years ago and is still in progress. The Hawaiian islands are the emergent tips of a range of volcanoes that reach altitudes of over 13,000 feet above sea-level and stretch across the Pacific for 1,,553 miles from north-east to south-east. When they first emerged from the ocean depths, the islands were composed of sterile volcanic rocks on which life developed over the course of millions of years. The archipelago's isolation from other areas of dry land resulted in an unusual form of biological colonisation with the sea and the winds bringing seeds and spores from diverse continents. According to the botanists, 1,300 endemic plant species developed from 260 initial spores, while for the biologists Hawaii beats even the Galapagos Islands for the number and variety of species to have evolved from a single common ancestor. On these 132 fragments of dry land scattered across the ocean, biological evolution has created 150 different ecosystems, from jungles to lagoons through to the 28 square miles of perennial ice on the summit of Mauna Kea (13,800 feet) which formed during the Ice Age. Man arrived from the neighboring Marquesas archipelago in the 4th century AD. On islands inhabited by large flightless birds that were easy prey, the Polynesians became hunters.

Although a brief visit was made in 1542 by the Italian Giovanni Gaetano in the service of the Spanish crown, the credit for the discovery of the Hawaiian Islands is attributed to James Cook in 1778. Here he was the first European to witness the Maoris, the original surfers, riding the waves balanced on wooden boards. The Hawaiian's considered Cook to be a god, but irritated by the behavior of the British crews they changed their minds and Cook was killed on February 14, 1779 during his third voyage. The arrival of the white men convinced the Hawaiians that their only hope for survival was to remain united, the task of bringing together the eight inhabited islands under a single ruler falling to Kamehameha I. In the meantime the archipelago was visited by unscrupulous adventurers, whalers, traders and missionaries. The priests' initial concerns were to clothe the islanders' sinful nudity and to repress the *hula*, ignoring the centuries of tradition that lay behind the provocative dance. For a number of decades they succeeded in covering the seductive bodies of the girls with shapeless shift-dresses and to forbid the *hula*, which was only revived in the late nineteenth century thanks to King Kalakaua.

Under the pressure of the American traders, the South Seas Island myth had already given way to the rules of business. In 1848, after having transferred the capital from Lahaina to Honolulu, King Kamehameha III passed the law of *mahele* abrogating the islands' traditional collective inheritance and introducing private property and the buying and selling of land. This marked the beginning of the Hawaiian ethnic and cultural decline as the islanders were dispossessed by American financial flattery and killed by western diseases. From Cook's arrival to the end of the nineteenth century, the population fell from 300,000 to 29,000 inhabitants. In 1887 the king conceded exclusive use of the natural port

86-87 *The spectacular rocky cliff of the Na Pali Coast falling sheer to the sea can be seen in this aerial photo. This, the island's wildest and most unspoilt stretch of coastline, is situated on its north-west side.*

86 bottom left *The coast of Kauai, an island on which the sheer cliffs of the north-west coast alternate with the beaches and caves eroded by the sea Haena Point. Hawaiian legend has it that the caves were excavated by the goddess Pele.*

86 bottom right *The Hawaiian Islands is the world's most isolated archipelago. The American coast is almost 2,500 miles away, Japan 2,400, Australia 5,000 and Antarctica 6,800. Hawaii's closest neighbours are the minuscule Marquesas Islands, 500 miles to the south.*

of Pearl Harbor to the United States. It was here that on December 7, 1941, the Japanese launched the air attack that extended the Second World War to the Pacific. By that time, most of the useful agricultural land had passed into white hands and the monarchy had been reduced to the role of a puppet whose strings were pulled by American businessmen. In response to Queen Li iuokalani's attempt to restore her status, Sanford Ballard Dole, the representative of the American government, overthrew the monarchy with the support of the marines and the following year was elected President of the Hawaiian Republic. In 1897, the archipelago was annexed by the United States and in 1959 became the fiftieth star on the flag of the Union.

The American colonization also had an environmental impact. The planet's most remarkable laboratory of biological evolution was devastated with the introduction of animals and crops from other continents. Pigs, cows and goats were imported in order to supply the crews of the nineteenth-century ships with meat. The logging industry destroyed great swathes of forest which were replaced with sugarcane, pineapple and guava plantations. Today the greater part of the archipelago's vegetation is composed of plants introduced by the colonizers.

The Hawaiian natives refused to work on the plantations and thus large-scale immigration from China, Japan and the Philippines began. The descendants of the Maoris now number just 10,000, less than 1% of the state's total population of 1,200,000, and they do not benefit from the "nation" status granted to the 308 American Indian tribes in the United States.

In the 1950s, the Hawaiian Islands became the dream destination for American holidaymakers and tourism is now the mainstay of the economy, with 7 million visitors landing each year, compared with the total of less than 1 million for all the other islands of Polynesia, Melanesia and Micronesia.

Hawaii is the state in which Americans plan to retire, thanks to the tropical climate, the beauty of the landscape and the laid-back lifestyle. Waikiki beach at Honolulu is thus blighted by groves of apartment blocks, shopping malls, highway junctions and thirty-floor hotels.

87 top This photo shows a volcanic peak on Kauai. Geologically speaking, this island is the oldest of the Hawaiian archipelago, as demonstrated by the rock strata of Waimea Canyon, a gorge over 3,000 feet deep and 9.5 miles long.

87 center Surfing, today the most popular sport in the Pacific Ocean, originated in the Hawaiian Islands, where in 1778 James Cook became the first European to see the

Polynesians riding the waves balanced on light wooden boards up to 16.5 feet long.

87 bottom Beaches are the key to the success of tourism in the Hawaiian Islands, where each year 7 million visitors land and where many American dream of retiring to, even though the cost of living is the highest in the United States and homes in Honolulu cost twice those in New York.

88 top A bay on the island of Hawaii can be seen in this photo. Pearl Harbor is to be found on the island of Oahu, the first part of the archipelago to be conceded by the king to United States in 1887 and the site of the Japanese aerial bombardment on December 7, 1941, that extended the Second World War to the Pacific.

88 center The first churches to appear in the Hawaiian archipelago were erected by the pastors of the London Missionary Society, who landed in the Polynesian archipelago in 1797, initiating a process of conversion to Christianity that resulted in the loss of aspects of Polynesian culture such as nudity, dance and tattooing.

88-89 This photo of Wailua falls gives an idea of the hydrogeological complexity of the interior of Kauai, an island with seven rivers cutting through rain-forests where rainbows are the norm, thanks to the frequent showers.

88 bottom The Hawaiian Islands are an extraordinary natural laboratory in which biological evolution created 150 different ecosystems from jungles - the photo shows the fertile coasts of Hawaii—to the lagoon and the 28 square miles of perennial ice at the top of Mauna Kea (13,800 feet) that formed during the Ice Age.

89 bottom The coastline of the
island of Kauai is composed of
cliffs and a number of magnificent
beaches, in particular Lumahai
Beach, the most frequently
photographed in the Hawaiian
Islands thanks to its immaculate
white sand that contrasts with the
black volcanic rock. This section of
coastline may lack beaches, but an
extraordinary coral reef can be
observed in the transparent waters.

90 top left The forested relief features of the island of Hawaii can be seen in this aerial photo. Big Island, as it is also known, is the most recently formed of the archipelago and with its 4,000 square miles accounts for two thirds of the total dry land.

90 center left Its distance from other areas of dry land meant that a unique biological development took place in the Hawaiian archipelago. From 260 initial spores 1,300 plant species eventually evolved, whilst in terms of fauna the Hawaiian Islands overtook even the Galapagos islands in terms of the number and variety of species generated from a common ancestor.

90 bottom left This aerial photo of the top of a volcano clearly shows that the Hawaiian Islands are actually the emergent peaks of a mountain range of seismic origins, extending for 1,550 miles from north-west to south-east in the northern section of the Pacific Ocean.

90 top right The island of Kauai was the scene of Captain James Cook's first Hawaiian landing on January 18, 1778. He baptized the archipelago the "Sandwich Islands" in honor of the First Lord of the British Admiralty and his patron, John Montague, Earl of Sandwich.

90 center right In the middle of the Tertiary Period the volcanoes of the Hawaiian Islands rose from the ocean depths through cracks in the earth's crust. This process produced the world's greatest mountain, Mauna Kea, which from the ocean floor to its peak rises almost 33,000 feet; that is to say, 3,300 feet more than Mount Everest. This photo shows a section of coastline of clearly volcanic origins on the island of Oahu.

91 The Hawaiian archipelago is the earth's youngest island group, the fruit of a seismic process that began 25 million years ago and continues its advance towards the south-east because the islands are situated on a mobile section of the Pacific Plate. A spectacular photo of an extraordinary lava flow from the Kilauea volcano on the island of Hawaii.

92 top *Easter Island was baptized by Jacob Roggeveen, who discovered it on Easter Day, 1722, during a voyage of exploration undertaken on behalf of the Dutch East Indies Company. Ovahe beach is seen here.*

92-93 *The moai of Easter Island were set with their backs turned to the sea and their eyes, made of black obsidian and white coral, staring at the village. From those eyes flowed* mana *or spiritual power, the positive energy that motivated the lives of men.*

Easter Island:

93 top Anakena beach, seen in this photo, was for centuries the customary landing point on Easter Island. Situated 12.5 miles to the north of Hanga Roa, the sleepy capital, it is today a national park frequented on Sundays by picnicking islanders.

93 bottom The moai were sculpted in the living rock of the hillsides from which they were gradually detached and slid towards their plinths on tree trunks. Some of the statues weighed up to 80 tons and their movement and raising required the labors of hundreds of men.

the navel of the world

The inhabitants of Easter Island call it "Te-Pito-O-Te-Henua", the Navel of the World. Situated 2,326 miles off the coast of South America and 2,515 miles from Papeete, a more isolated island would be difficult to find. A place of myth and legend fuelled by unsolved mysteries and the geographical and cultural outpost of the inhabited world, Easter Island is a 63-square-mile wedge of black volcanic rock in the middle of the blue ocean. It was baptized by the Dutch navigator Jacob Roggeveen, who discovered it on Easter Day, 1722. This is the island of the moai, the 886 anthropomorphic statues scattered across the barren hills. Monolithic blocks of volcanic tuff of between 6.5 and 72 feet in height, the largest being the incomplete Great Moai which is still locked into the living rock from which it was sculpted on the south face of the volcano Rano Raraku, the source of the stone for the statues and the site of their carving. Almost 500 moai were completed and hoisted onto ceremonial terraces known as ahu, their heads covered with pukao, top-knots of red stone. Today, most of the monuments lie on the ground badly damaged, but a few dozen of the upright statues still dominate the landscape, their backs turned towards the sea and their eyes, in black obsidian and white coral, staring at the villages. It was from the eyes of the moai that flowed the mana, the spiritual power. Another 400 statues lie incomplete on the slopes and in the craters of the volcano. Who sculpted the moai, how and why?

This enigma fascinated the early explorers and has fed a series of improbable hypotheses involving extraterrestrials, the lost continent of Mu and an island cemetery for the whole of Polynesia. There are instead no doubts as to the origins of the inhabitants of Easter Island, the southernmost heirs of the Polynesian diaspora as confirmed by DNA examinations performed on burial remains. Archaeological relics have dated human presence on the island to 620 AD. The Rapanui, the inhabitants of the island which is also known as Rapa Nui meaning Big Rock, are distinguished from other Maori groups by their large pierced ear lobes. Legend has it that it was the demi-god Hotu Matu'a who led the migration from Hiva aboard two canoes that, as well as dozens of men, also carried dogs, chickens, turtles, and banana, taro, yam, sandalwood and hibiscus plants. This legend reinforces the hypothesis of a migration from the Marquesas group where three islands are called Hiva. An aura of magical mystery still surrounds the history of this people and its decline. Having reached the island the clan settled on volcanic terrain lacking bays and coral reefs but covered with forests and with a

maximum elevation of 1,840 feet. An agricultural civilization developed that, thanks to the rains and the fertile soil, permitted a reasonable standard of living to be achieved. This was the first phase of the colonization of Rapa Nui, the Ahu Moai, from the name of the great statues; a millennium characterized by a theocratic equilibrium that resulted in peace amongst the clans, stability in the means of production and the crystallization of social norms. The Rapanui, unique among the Polynesian peoples, developed a form of hieroglyphic writing known as rongo rongo which they incised on wooden tablets from right to left and from left to right on successive lines. The system was decoded in 1996 by the American researcher Steven Fischer.

The lifestyle of the Rapanui was not very different to that of the other Maoris until the construction of the moai became the principal activity and absorbed all their energy and the resources of the island. The sculptures were carved into the rock of the hillsides, from where they were detached and dragged towards their plinths using tree-trunks. Some of the moai weighed up to 80 tons and their transportation required hundreds of men and the felling of thousands of trees. The constructive frenzy of the theocrats led to the total deforestation of the island which in turn provoked an environmental crisis with consequent social and cultural implications. Having reached Rapa Nui, the most remote of the inhabited islands, the Polynesians apparently lost their navigational instinct and the migrations southwards undertaken by some groups were unsuccessful. Thus was interrupted a pattern that had functioned as a demographic regulator in the rest of Polynesia. Their seafaring knowledge having been lost, the Rapanui remained trapped on the island.

94-95 This photo of an enormous crater demonstrates that Easter Island too has volcanic origins. The island is situated midway between Tahiti and Chile (to which it belongs politically) while the nearest land is Pitcairn Island, 1,300 miles to the west.

94 bottom and 95 top Rather improbably, Rapa Nui takes on the appearance of a Southern Seas paradise island in this photo of Anakena beach. The palms were planted by colonists as the island had been completely deforested as a result of the felling of trees for the transportation and raising of the moai.

The population increased exponentially despite the increasingly restricted resources, inevitably leading to the total collapse of any form of equilibrium. Thus began the second historical period, the *Huri Moai*. The demographic explosion provoked tribal warfare and the *moai* sculptures were demolished and replaced by the cult of the Tangata Manu, the Bird-Man, and the Make-Make, the ancient god of war. These conflicts were used as the background for the film *"Rapa Nui"* (1994) starring Kevin Costner and directed by Kevin Reynolds. In the 17th century the war declined into a hopeless spiral as the last remaining forests were burned, the fields were ruined and the population was decimated.

Roggeveen, Cook and La Pérouse, the European explorers who reached Rapa Nui in the eighteenth century, found a denuded island with two thousand inhabitants living naked and undernourished in the bizarre setting of toppled *moai*. The contact with the white men triggered yet another catastrophe as the population was once again decimated by smallpox and venereal disease, while slave ships transported the fitter natives to work on the guano islands. When in 1888 Rapa Nui was acquired by the Chilean government which undertook to prevent further deportations, only around a hundred native Rapanui remained. Colonized by Hispanic peoples, Easter Island now has a population of 2,800.

95 bottom By the time the European explorers discovered the island, Rapa Nui had been completely deforested. In their frenzy to construct the moai, the natives had felled all the trees, provoking an environmental crisis that soon had social and cultural implications. A group of wild horses grazes on the slopes of the Rano Raraku volcano in this photo.

96 top Fua'amotu beach is one of the many to be found on the south-east coast of Tongatapu, the largest of the islands in the Kingdom of Tonga. They are all banks of white sand deriving from the erosion of the coral reefs surrounding the island.

96 center The 'Utula 'Aina promontory composed of a neck of land covered in vegetation is to be found on the northern coast of Vava'u, an island with an extremely complex coastline featuring profound bays such as Port of Refuge, considered to be one of the safest anchorages during the hurricane season.

96 bottom This photo shows an atoll in the Ha'apai island group. The Kingdom of Tonga is composed of four archipelagos (Tongatapu, Ha'apai, Vava'u and Niuas) comprising a total of 170 islands (only 36 are inhabited). The majority are volcanic in origin, but many were formed as a result of the action of coral polyps.

97 One of the many coral reefs extending between the archipelagos of Ha'apai and Vava'u in the Kingdom of Tonga. A flight between these two groups of islands and the capital Nuku'alofa is one of the most spectacular in the Pacific.

Tonga: the contradictory world of a bygone kingdom

A kingdom dating back to 950 AD which conquered parts of Fiji and Samoa, Tonga is the only archipelago to have never been colonized. Legend has it that the Tu'i Tonga, the native sovereigns, are of divine origin. Today, there is probably no one who still believes this myth, but Tupou IV is nonetheless one of the last absolute monarchs. The king possesses the land and in a feudal system concedes plots to the adult males, reserving a third of the territory for himself and the families of related aristocrats. In spite of the name "Friendly Islands", with which James Cook baptized the archipelago after landing in the Tongatapu group in 1773, for the two successive centuries the Kingdom of Tonga was distinguished by the indifference, not to say suspicion, with which it treated foreigners. Following the arrival of Abel Tasman in 1643, the first European to set foot on the islands, the white men were nicknamed *palangi*, or "exploded from the sky" as according to the Tongans it was impossible to cross the Pacific and therefore their ships must have descended from the stars. After the initial contacts, however, the islanders withdrew into the *faka-Tonga* or traditional way of life which is still conserved today with the interweaving of relationships within the extended family, archaic items of clothing such as the *to'ovala* (a straw belt handed down through the generations) and the devotion to the crown. The missionaries took decades to convert the Tongans but once they had adopted Christianity they became one of the most puritan peoples of Oceania. Still today it is a crime for men to appear in public bare-chested and those who work on Sunday, breaking the biblical law of the day of rest, are liable to be arrested. In the difficult balance between tradition and faith, dance has remained the liveliest of the arts. The dancers with the costumes of grasses and their skins coated with coconut oil move gracefully, miming the words of the songs. At the end of the performance they are rewarded by the audience with banknotes stuck to their greasy bodies.

Nuku'alofa, the capital, is a sleepy, dusty city. Thanks to

17 feet high and weighing over eight tons. Certain archaeologists attribute these monuments to the Lapita civilization that flourished between 1500 and 500 BC. Carbon 14 testing has dated some remains to 1100 BC, whilst the presence of man has been dated to 3000 BC. Tongatapu, which means Sacred South, was the capital of the Lapita people, with its lagoon acting as the naval base and southerly tip of their empire. It was here that with the encounter between the Melanesians and the peoples from China, Indochina and the Philippines that the linguistic and physical characteristics of the proto-Polynesians were defined.

While Tongatapu contains the history of Polynesia, the rest of the archipelago illustrates the variety of its landscapes. Situated immediately to the west of the International Date Line, Tonga is composed of 170 islands (36 of which are inhabited by a total population of 110,000) grouped in four archipelagos (Tongatapu, Ha'apai, Vava'u and Niuas) accounting for a total land area of 289 square miles, distributed in an area of ocean as vast as Great Britain and Ireland. Tongatapu is itself a large, flat rocky island with a complex coastline that overlooks a lagoon studded with minuscule atolls and also comprises 'Eua, a mountainous island whose plateaus have Savannah-like vegetation. Around 620 miles to the north, fifty or so atolls with coral reefs, blue lagoons and the active volcanoes of Tofua and Kao, form the Ha'apai archipelago, linked to the northernmost group of Vava'u by slivers of sand and coral that make a flight over the islands of Tonga one of the most spectacular in the Pacific. Vava'u is composed of a principal island of calcareous rock cloaked in forests with long, lacy arms embracing a lagoon dotted with 72 small dome-shaped islands covered with vegetation that resemble the Micronesian landscape of Palau. This labyrinth of hilly islands with beaches and inlets, together with the deep bay of Port of Refuge which offers protection even from hurricanes, has transformed Vava'u into a popular sailing resort. Much further north, three volcanic cones compose the forgotten and virtually uninhabited Niuas archipelago.

98-99 The Fofoa lagoon offers a typical Vava'u landscape. The archipelago is composed of a principal island (with dozens of promontories, peninsulas and deep bays) surrounded by 72 hilly islets covered with luxuriant tropical vegetation.

98 bottom The Royal Palace of Tongatapu stands on the sea front at Nuku'alofa. The prefabricated wooden building was actually made in New Zealand in 1867. Tonga boasts the oldest monarchy in the Pacific which can trace its roots back to 950 AD and has extended its power over parts of Fiji and Samoa.

99 top The clothes worn by this Tongan nobleman are typical of Tongan society, the most traditional in Polynesia, where even the court aristocracy wear a to'ovala, the broad belt of straw and coconut fiber which supports the traditional skirt, along with their jacket and tie.

99 bottom The Trilithon is one of the most important archaeological sites of the Pacific. The megalithic arch is composed of three blocks of coralline rock, each weighing around 50 tons. It is located to the east of Tongatapu and was erected in the 13th century by the sovereign, Tu'i Tatui.

the money earned by many Tongans through the cultivation of marrows for the Japanese market during the last decade, the main road has filled with haphazardly parked cars. The center of activity is, however, still the market where westerners are disorientated by the variety of tropical fruit and above all the root vegetables related to the taro, manioc and sweet potato. The city is dominated by the Victorian-style royal palace on the sea front where the Tongans stroll with open umbrellas to shade themselves from the sun, only to close them at the first sign of rain to enjoy a cooling shower. In the north-east of Tongatapu stands Mu'a, the first home of the Tu'i Tonga. At Lapaha, one and a half miles away, the kings lie buried in 28 pyramids constructed with blocks of coral on three levels. The monument that makes Tonga one of the most important archaeological sites in the Pacific is, however, the Ha'amonga'a at Maui Trilithon, a kind of megalithic dolmen composed of three gigantic blocks of coral almost

100-101 *Return to Paradise beach, situated on the south coast of Upolu (Western Samoa), was the natural location for the film of that name directed in 1952 by Mark Robson and starring Gary Cooper. The film was an adaptation of a story in Tales of the South Pacific by James Michener.*

100 bottom *Apia is the capital of Western Samoa. A pleasant coastal town with an attractive church (seen here) and the liveliest market in the Southern Seas. The writer Robert Louis Stevenson lived and died in a house at Vailima in the hills surrounding the town.*

Composed of nine islands drenched by an equatorial climate, Samoa is the mythical Hawaiki, the cradle of the Polynesian civilization. The most reliable myth regarding the peopling of the Pacific recounts that, around 300 AD, migrations departed from the island of Savaii that led the Maori to colonize the most distant islands of the Southern Seas. Faithful to its role as a treasure-chest of tradition, Samoa, or at least the independent islands that form the state of Western Samoa, is the archipelago that has best conserved Polynesian customs and lifestyle. A rather different scenario is encountered on Tutuila, the largest of the islands in American Samoa; in this corner of Polynesia over which fly the Stars and Stripes, the beauty of the landscape blends with western prosperity and the odors from the tuna canning factories. The home of an American naval base since 1872, Tutuila was annexed

Samoa: the cradle of the maori civilization

by the United States in 1900 following an agreement regarding control over the area reached with Britain and Germany. Governed as an autonomous territory, American Samoa enjoys the privilege of being a free port and its economy is bolstered by the money sent back by emigrant workers in California and Hawaii as well as by the canning industry. The deep bay of Pago Pago—the territorial capital where Somerset Maugham set his story *Rain*—is one of the most spectacular in Oceania with precipitous mountains buried in jungle vegetation that terminate in cliffs falling sheer to the sea. In search of the roots of Polynesia we return to the dreamy western islands of Upolu and Savaii which were populated by the Lapita people—the proto-Polynesian civilization—from Tonga and Fiji around 1500 BC. The remains of a Lapita village discovered on Upolu date back to 1000 BC. Around a thousand years ago, Tonga, then the most powerful kingdom in the region, invaded Savaii and unsuccessfully attempted to conquer Upolu. There followed a treaty that guaranteed peace between the two archipelagos until the arrival of de Bougainville in 1768. The French explorer reinforced the Maori myth of Hawaiki by calling Samoa the "Navigator Archipelago", due to the extraordinary ability with which the natives tackled the ocean aboard minuscule canoes. In contrast with Tonga, the only archipelago governed by a strong centralized power, Samoa was overwhelmed by the colonizers. In the second half of the nineteenth century, competition between the *aiga*, the extended families on which Samoa society is based, for the nomination of the great *matai*, the chief of chiefs and holder of supreme power, exploded in conflict between two rival dynasties. This opportunity was exploited by the Germans who acquired land in exchange for arms, laying the basis for its future colony. Regaining its independence in 1962—after having been passed from Germany to Great Britain and finally to New Zealand—Western Samoa is now the archipelago in which Polynesian traditions are strongest. Situated on a large bay, the capital Apia is the only city and it features concrete buildings, bustling markets and traffic (composed of brightly colored, long-nosed buses blasting out reggae music) conducted by policemen wearing the *lava-lava* (the traditional skirt) and colonial helmets. The rest of the population—the inhabitants of the two states together number 230,000 in an area of 1,210 square miles—live in villages composed of *fale*, huts made of wood and coconut fronds, furnished with beds and equipped with electricity but without walls. This type of construction is due to the

extremely humid climate of the archipelago as well as the absence of a need for privacy. The village frequently corresponds with an *aiga*, the extended family led by a *matai*, that remains the fulcrum of Samoan society even though it is no longer the autarchic community it was in the past. The wealth of the *aiga*—measured in terms of cars and modern electrical appliances—derives from the savings sent back by family members emigrated to New Zealand and representing four-fifths of the economy of Western Samoa. The simplicity of the Samoan lifestyle captivated the Scottish writer Robert Louis Stevenson, who had a house built at Vailima, in the hills behind Apia, where he spent his last years. From Vailima one can enjoy a spectacular view over the landscape of Upolu, a volcanic island cloaked with forests that cover half of its surface area, with thrusting peaks and volcanoes eroded over time that descend towards the coast in gently sloping plains. The shoreline is rimmed with towering coconut palms shading long beaches of white sand. The large island of Savaii, separated from Upolu by the strait containing the smaller islands of Apolima and Manono, is even wilder. A rough road traces the perimeter of the island, linking the scattered coastal villages, whilst the interior—covered with dense rain-forest interrupted by a number of powerful waterfalls—features around 20 volcanoes, some of which are still active. The 6,068-foot Mount Silisili is the highest point on the island. The more recently formed Savaii has frequently been shaken by violent eruptions and on the north coast one can find lunar landscapes modelled by vast lava flows.

101 top The interiors of Upolu and Savaii, the two main islands of Western Samoa, are covered with luxuriant tropical vegetation, slashed in places by dramatic waterfalls. Many homes have been built in the shade of spectacular flamboyants (in the photo)

101 bottom The Aleipata beaches on the south-east coast of Upolu, opposite the island of Nu'utele, offer some of the most evocative scenery in Western Samoa. Traditional villages stand on the sea shore with the fale *(huts) constructed without walls.*

two by a footpath snaking through the aerial roots of the fig trees, lianas and arboreal ferns. An island like many others were it not for the legend of the Yankee, the brig was used in the 1950s by *National Geographic* magazine for reports throughout the world until it struck the coral reef and sank off Avarua in 1964. All that remains of the wreck today are a few rusty plates that emerge at low tide, but in the port of Avarua, observing the loading of the decrepit merchant ships departing for the atolls of the Northern Group, one is immediately immersed in the myth of the Southern Seas.

The Cook Islands are divided into the rather unimaginatively named Northern and Southern Groups. The northern archipelago is culturally less homogeneous—many islands have Samoan linguistic influences—but more uniform from a

Cook Islands: the dreamy archipelago on the edge of time

Rarotonga is the garden-island of the Pacific, drenched in the perfume of hibiscus, gardenias, frangipani, flamboyants and orchids, a cocktail of aromas intensified by the warm, damp climate. It is best experienced by following the Ara Metua, the road twisting through the interior, amidst papaya, banana and cotton plantations, past giant mangoes and an orgy of multicolored flowers. It runs parallel to Are Tapu, the 20-mile coast road tracing the perimeter of Rarotonga, the principal island of the fifteen composing an archipelago-state of just 20,000 inhabitants. Together, the islands account for 93 square miles of dry land, lost in 772,000 square miles of ocean. An independent microcosm, in spite of its association with New Zealand in matters of defence and foreign policy, situated mid-way between Tahiti and Samoa. The interior of Rarotonga is dominated by volcanic peaks and is cloaked in rain forest, cut in

morphological perspective. It is composed of coral atolls with tongues of white sand covered with palms that enclose turquoise lagoons.

Manihiki is the most beautiful of the atolls with forty *motus* (small coral islands) surrounding a lagoon in which black pearls are cultivated. A trip through the southern archipelago instead provides a synthesis of Polynesian geology. There is the young Rarotonga, still dominated by volcanic cones albeit now extinct, and the lagoon atolls of Palmerston and Aitutaki. This last is the only island in the Cook archipelago to be part of the international tourism circuit, thanks to one of the most magnificent lagoons in the Pacific surrounded by 21 *motus* of immaculate sand. Then there are the archaic Mangaia, Atiu, Mitiaro, Mauke, Manuae and Takutea, *makatea* islands formed 10 million years ago with substrates of calcareous rock of coralline origin, lakes and grottoes with stalactites and stalagmites. These islands present the wildest side of the archipelago, with interiors cloaked in dense vegetation and coastlines featuring cliffs alternating with deserted beaches, such as Onovaru, where James Cook, the British navigator after whom the archipelago is named, landed in 1777.

On Rarotonga, one may sit on the terrace of Trader Jacks in the capital Avarua and listen to the sea-faring stories of the skippers who gather to drink rivers of beer as the setting sun sets the bay aflame. With its grindingly hot days and lazy evenings, Avarua epitomizes the indolence of the Southern Seas. It comes to life only on Friday nights when the laid-back band at Trader Jacks is flanked by the dance rhythms of Banana Court and the Empire cinema, in part used as a laundry, is transformed into a discoteque. With public transport and services that actually work, the lazy Cook Islands appear to be one of the most westernized corners of Polynesia, but they still retain numerous traditional elements. Maori culture survives in sculpture and religious art and in dance which is taught every day in the school courtyard. Land and houses belong to the clans who distribute them to their members according to their needs. This is a controversial practice as on the one hand there is no building speculation, but on the other development is discouraged and emigration has become a problem. As in other archipelagoes, the

102 top This photo shows the area of Avarua housing the University of the South Pacific, the library, the 1842 Takaloa Mission and the Taurnanga Vanaga Cook Islands Cultural Center, the multi-media complex that in 1992 housed the Festival of Pacific Arts.

102 bottom Avarua, the capital of the Cook Islands, situated on the north coast of Rarotonga is seen in this aerial photo. This is one of the sleepiest cities in the Southern Seas, with a few commercial centers, a couple of bars and an old port from which mail boats depart for the rest of the archipelago.

most important factor in the economy is the money sent back by workers in New Zealand, where more islanders now live than remain on the islands themselves. Looking beyond the picture postcard image, Rarotonga is on the threshold of bankruptcy due to an economic policy that is overly generous in relation to the meager gross national product. Nobody on the island seems to be worried, however. They never lost their sang-froid, even when in 1996, in order to tackle the overwhelming foreign debt, the government halved state salaries. A return to a subsistence economy is unthinkable despite the showmen of the cultural villages and Piri who attempt to illustrate how the islanders could live on coconuts alone. The standard of living is western, with traffic composed largely of enduro-type motorcycles, frequently ridden by large Polynesian ladies wearing nothing but a pareo (the same ladies who on Sundays can be found wearing pretty lace hats and singing the praises of the Lord in the Cook Islands Christian Church). Heirs of the Maori navigators who reached the archipelago from the legendary Hawaiki, the islanders combine the faith imported by the missionaries with Polynesian myths. Little or nothing remains of the *marae*, the spiritual meeting places, but statues of Tangaroa (the god of the sea and creation) equipped with a huge phallus are ubiquitous. And ancestors continue to be buried in the courtyards of the houses.

102-103 This aerial photo shows the coast at Muri on Rarotonga (Cook Islands), the most spectacular stretch of coastline on the island with the coral reef enclosing a transparent lagoon, a number of islets and beaches of white sand rimmed by towering palms.

103 bottom The inhabitants of the Cook Islands number around 20,000, but a similar number of Polynesians originally from the archipelago now live in Auckland. The Cook Islands are an independent state but associated with New Zealand with regards to defence and foreign policy.

104 top The Aitutaki lagoon is one of the most beautiful in Polynesia thanks to its transparent depths, exalted by the immaculate sand, in which turtles and brilliantly colored tropical fish can be observed along with a pelagic fauna that includes tunas, marlins and barracudas.

104-105 Tapuaetai offers the enchanting landscape of Aitutaki, one of the Cook Islands formed from the submerged crater of a volcano enclosed within a coral reef from which 21 motu of white sand studded with palm trees have emerged.

104 bottom Here the photographer has lingered over the enchanted setting of Motu Maina, the most spectacular coral islet of Aitutaki. A long tongue of pure white sand extends into the blue lagoon. In the waters off the motu lies the wreck of a boat that sank in 1930.

105 bottom The interior of Rarotonga is composed of mountains of volcanic origins, largely covered with jungle vegetation, whilst the flat land has been cultivated with papaya. The abundant rains have transformed the island into a natural garden decorated with hibiscus of various colors.

MICRONESIA: GREEN MOUNTAINS IN A BLUE OCEAN

various archipelagos, Micronesian is used to describe a race originating from the meeting of the Negro peoples arriving from Papua New Guinea—around 1,000 years before Christ—and the peoples migrating from Indonesia, the Philippines and southern China. The typical Micronesian is of average build and stature, with golden skin, straight, black hair and almond-shaped eyes. Nine languages are officially spoken in Micronesia, all belonging to the Austronesian stock, although in reality English is used ever more frequently today and the life-style of the islanders is ever more western in style. This is because in Micronesia, as in the Hawaiian Islands, the influence of the European colonists was much stronger than in Polynesia and Melanesia. Following Magellan's landing in the Marianas in 1521, the Spanish controlled the region until 1885. Guam, the largest of the Micronesian islands with a surface area of 212 square miles, had been for hundreds of years an important staging post for the Spanish galleons on the route between the Philippines and Mexico. With the collapse of the Spanish colonial empire in the late nineteenth century, Germany acquired control over the Marianas, Marshall and Caroline Islands for 25 million pesetas whilst the United States appropriated the port of Guam. Following the German defeat in the First World War, the German archipelagos came under Japanese control. During the Second World War, Micronesia became the theater of furious air and naval battles between the Americans and the Japanese. Following their bloody conquest of the region, island by island, fighting to the last man, the Americans transformed Micronesia, lying just 1,860 miles from Japan, into the air base from which they destroyed the Empire of the Rising Sun. On the 6th of August, 1945, *Enola Gay*, the aircraft that dropped the atomic bomb on Hiroshima and thus brought an end to the war, took off from the island of Tinian in the Marianas. In 1947 the Marianas, Caroline and Marshall archipelagos came under the sovereignty of the United States which installed numerous military bases considered to be of strategic importance in controlling the Pacific. Wake Island, today claimed by the Marshall Islands, became an air base for the American navy. Micronesia still had a further role to play in the history of atomic warfare as the Americans transformed the Marshall Islands atolls of Bikini and Eniwetok into nuclear firing ranges: up to the 1950s dozens of tests were carried out with atomic and thermonuclear devices.

106 top The republic of Kiribati is composed of 33 coral atolls straddling the Equator. Its 83,000 inhabitants conduct the most traditional of Micronesian lifestyles with a subsistence economy based on fishing and tropical agriculture.

106 center The Kayangel atoll is situated in the northernmost part of the republic of Palau. It is composed of four islands with palm trees and white beaches and a barrier reef surrounding a lagoon inhabited by manta rays, leopard sharks and sea turtles among myriad other species.

106 bottom The 2,141 fragments of land that form this region alternate with hundreds of coral reefs (seen here in this aerial photo).

107 The Rock Islands are actually uplifted reef structures cloaked in luxuriant emerald green vegetation that seem to float in the deep blue of the ocean.

Micronesia translates as "small islands," an appropriate name for the world's most Lilliputian geographical region. Including all the rocks of volcanic origin and the coral atolls there are 2,141 fragments of land cloaked in vegetation thanks to the warm, damp climate. Only a hundred or so of these fragments are inhabited. Together they account for an area of dry land of just 1,240 square miles, little more than the surface area of Luxembourg, scattered across 3,860,000 square miles of ocean, an area as vast as the whole of the United States, Alaska included. Micronesia is composed of the Marianas, Caroline, Marshall and Kiribati archipelagos and the Nauru atoll, all situated on or to the north of the equator, half-way between the Hawaiian Islands and the Philippines. Apart from Kiribati and Nauru, both independent republics within the ambit of the British Commonwealth, the archipelagos have political ties of one form or another with the United States. With the exception of Nauru, which is rich in phosphates, the other state-archipelagos live largely thanks to aid from abroad—in particular from the United States—with imports exceeding exports by twenty to thirty times to compensate for the otherwise austere local economies based on tropical agriculture, fishing and a little tourism. The Micronesian population—a total of 420,000 inhabitants—has diverse ethnic origins according to the various islands. Here the influence of the migrations from neighboring Asia is much stronger than in other Oceanic regions, as testified by the features of the inhabitants of the small islands. Leaving aside the ethnic differences between the

108 top The volcanic islands of the Palau archipelago are surrounded by coral reefs that contribute to breathtaking scenery. The reefs are incredibly complex ecosystems with submarine holes and caverns in which over 1,000 species of fish and 700 different corals have been identified.

108-109 The island of Ngemelis, in the Republic of Palau, features one of the world's most famous coral walls with a vertical rise of 790 feet. In this extensive reef, the madrepores have the most varied forms and colors: from the red of the gorgonia fans to the green of veritable coral trees through to the purples of the soft corals. In this photo, the separation between the shallow turquoise waters of the lagoon and the blue depths of the ocean can clearly be seen.

109 top The extraordinary landscape of the Rock Islands was produced as a result of the eruptions of a submarine volcano that, millions of years ago, wrecked a coral reef, creating hundreds of hilly rocks that appear mirage-like to float on the sea.

109 bottom This aerial photo shows the maze of green hills and watery channels of the rock island at Palau. The islets, in the form of domes, are composed of calcareous rock of coralline origin. Caverns opening in the rock walls lead to internal lakes.

Guide to the archipelagos

The Marianas is the northernmost of the Micronesian archipelagos consisting of Guam and 14 less important islands, arranged in an arc stretching 1,240 miles from the Philippines. Including Guam, the islands have a total surface area of 368 square miles. The southernmost islands are coral atolls whilst those to the north—situated on the Ring of Fire—are the upper reaches of a mountain range of volcanic origin that due to the phenomenon of subduction (where one tectonic plate slides under another) plunges into the Mariana Trench, also known as the Vitjaz Abyss (36,152 feet). The Chamorros, the inhabitants of the Marianas are the result of the amalgamation of the Micronesians, Asians and Spaniards: over centuries of contacts with the Spanish, Japanese and Americans they have lost the customs, rituals and traditions of Micronesia and are now Catholics, speak English and have western lifestyles. With 800 volcanic islands, rocks and coral atolls scattered over an area almost 1,900 miles long and 380 broad, the Caroline Islands represent the most extensive archipelago in the whole of Oceania. This is actually somewhat misleading as the majority of the tiny islands are uninhabited and the total surface area amounts to just 460 square miles. The population of 145,000 people, mostly of Micronesian origin, mainly inhabits the volcanic islands. In spite of their minuscule dimensions the Caroline Islands are divided into two distinct political entities. To the west is the Republic of Palau, also known as Belau, around 200 islands administered by the United States through the Trust Territory of the Pacific Islands. Its 17,000 inhabitants belong to Polynesian, Melanesian and Malayan stocks. The Rock Islands of Palau present one of the world's most extraordinary landscapes with hundreds of hilly, verdant islets that appear to float in the blue of the ocean. Some of these emerald hillocks enclose brilliant blue lagoons in stunning chromatic contrasts. The Rock Islands are surrounded by coral reefs in which 700 varieties of madrepores have been catalogued along with over a thousand species of fish, an authentic paradise for divers. It is no coincidence that Palau is the only Micronesian archipelago to boast a well-developed tourist industry. The 607 eastern Caroline Islands are instead divided into four states, Ponape, Truk, Yap and Kosrae, together forming the Federated States of Micronesia and inhabited principally by Micronesians although some islands have Polynesian populations. Located mid-way between the Hawaiian Islands and Papua New Guinea (to the north-east of the Caroline Islands), the minuscule Marshall Islands have a surface area of just 70 square miles distributed among 33 atolls with lagoons set along two parallel longitudinal axes, the eastern Ratak Chain, the Aurora Islands and the western Ralik Chain, the Sunset Islands. The 57,000 inhabitants are of Micronesian origins.

The inhabitants of the republic of Kiribati have conserved the lifestyle closest to the traditions of Micronesia as a whole: they live in huts and have a subsistence economy based on fishing and tropical agriculture. In reality the state budget is boosted by the cession of fishing rights to the Japanese fishing industry. The archipelago is composed of 33 atolls arranged in a horseshoe on the equator. The total dry land amounts to 277 square miles on which 83,000 people live. As well as the Gilbert Islands, Kiribati also includes the Phoenix Islands, the Line Islands (once known as the Equatorial Sporades) and Banaba (formerly Ocean Island). Located practically on the Equator, Nauru is an atoll-state of just 8.2 square miles. In reality it is a *makatea* island (with a substrate of coralline limestone) inhabited by no less than 10,000 people, half of whom are Micronesian and the remainder European and Chinese who came here to exploit one of the greatest phosphate deposits in the Pacific. Unfortunately, the extraction of this resource has led to the desertification of much of the island, confining the inhabitants to a 490-9840 foot broad green belt along the shore.

110-111 Micronesia boasts some of the Pacific's most beautiful beaches. The region is composed of the Marianas, Caroline, Marshall and Kiribati archipelagos as well as the Nauru atoll. The island groups are situated on the equator, midway between the Hawaiian Islands and the Philippines.

110 bottom left The center of social life on Yap in the Federated States of Micronesia is the faluw, *the house of men, seen here in this photo. The hut, built entirely of palm logs, cords, branches and fibers, acts as a school and a community center.*

110 bottom right The disc that can be seen in this photo is the ancient coinage of the island of Yap in the Federated States of Micronesia. These wheels of stone have a central hole and vary from 19.5 inches to 13 feet in diameter. In spite of their bulk and weight they were frequently transported from one island to another in canoes.

111 top The interiors of the islands composing the state of Yap (located in the eastern Caroline Islands) is covered with a dense jungle slashed by spectacular waterfalls. Palm-rimmed beaches alternate on the coasts with intricate mangroves.

111 bottom The state of Yap is composed of four islands (Maap, Tamil, Gagil and Yap) linked to one another by bridges, 130 atolls (including Ulithi with a lagoon covering an area of 209 square miles) and the island of Rumung which is instead only accessible by sea.

112 top As well as the large atoll of the same name, the state of Truk (associated with the Federated States of Micronesia) is composed of the Hall and Mortlock archipelagos, the island of Houk and the western atolls of Puluwat, Pulap and Namonuito. All the islands are covered with dense tropical vegetation.

112 bottom The lagoon of Truk has a perimeter of 140 miles. Boats can enter it via five navigable channels. In the eastern Caroline Islands where the state of Truk is located, some of the world's tallest varieties of palms can be found.

113 The state of Truk is constituted by around 300 islands, half of which are in the eastern Caroline Islands. Truk, the principal island, is an immense atoll composed of seven coralline islands and one of the world's largest lagoons with a surface area of 822 square miles.

114 top Amidst the coral of the Truk lagoon can be found a veritable submarine war museum with the rusting remains of ships, aircrafts, machine-guns and tanks. After a clean-up operation that lasted over twenty years, the atoll was designated as a national park. A diver explores the prow of a ship completely covered with numerous coral formations and sponges.

114 bottom Coral growing among the corroded wreck of the Japanese ship Fujikawa. The formations of coral, sea-fans and sea anemones, combined with the most extraordinary submarine collection of war relics, have transformed the Truk lagoon into one of the world's premier diving sites.

114-115 The lagoon of Truk was the theater in 1944 of one of the bloodiest battles of the Second World War. The size of the atoll—it has a diameter of 26 miles—allowed the Japanese to put up a fierce resistance to the attacks of the American navy. This photo captures something of the drama of the bombardments.

115 bottom This photo shows the remains of a ship in the lagoon surrounding Truk. In two air and naval attacks between February and April, 1944, the American sank 60 ships and shot down 420 aircrafts. The Japanese forces stationed on the atoll only surrendered a year later, however.

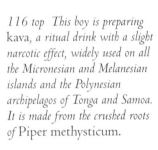

116 top This boy is preparing kava, a ritual drink with a slight narcotic effect, widely used on all the Micronesian and Melanesian islands and the Polynesian archipelagos of Tonga and Samoa. It is made from the crushed roots of Piper methysticum.

116 botton Throughout the Pacific the consumption of kava is frequently associated with rituals. The active ingredient of this drug derives from a combination of a dozen alkaloids attributed with anaesthetic, antibacterial, diuretics, aphrodisiac and magical powers.

116-117 Ponape, the largest island in the Federated States of Micronesia, is inhabited by Micronesian peoples. This is one of the most spectacular Pacific islands with a mountainous interior cloaked with forests of flowers and spice plants interrupted by 40 waterfalls. In this photo a group of children and young women wearing the typical garlands of flowers are playing traditional music.

117 bottom The vast majority of the 145,000 inhabitants of the Caroline Islands are of Micronesian origins. They live above all on the volcanic islands of an archipelago accounting for just 460 square miles of dry land but which are scattered across a stretch of ocean almost 1,900 miles long and 380 wide.

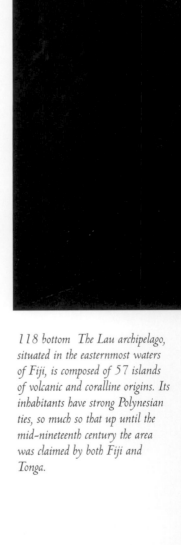

The first European navigators to land in this immense region of islands in the seventeenth century named it Melanesia; that is to say the "Black Islands," because it was inhabited by Negro peoples. Melanesia is composed of around 2,000 islands that, from New Guinea trace an immense crescent shape in the Pacific Ocean to the east of the Coral Sea. As well as the two parts into which New Guinea is divided (the Indonesian territory of Irian Jaya and the independent state Papua New Guinea), the region is composed of the archipelago state of the Solomon Islands, Vanuatu and Fiji and the French territory of New Caledonia. Much of Melanesia rests on the Ring of Fire, the chain of volcanoes located on the line of convergence between the Pacific and Indo-Australian plates. Off Vanuatu the meeting of the two tectonic plates has led to the creation of the New Hebrides Trench, a submarine abyss over 26,000 feet deep. Many of the Melanesian islands rise with the immense fold that from the highlands of New Guinea to New Zealand's North Island, forms the terrestrial crust of the western side of the Pacific.

The Melanesian islands share a warm, wet climate favoring the growth of vegetation, with coconut palms on the coasts and tropical rain forests inland. In all cases the eastern seaboards are the most luxuriant as the Trade Winds bring frequent rain. This is a region of intense volcanic activity and while most of the cones in New Guinea are extinct, many of the 600 islands scattered to the east of Papua are dominated by fiery craters.

The entire length of New Britain is studded with a series of volcanoes culminating in the 8,003-foot Mount Sinewit. The neighboring New Ireland has flat coastal areas while inland there are granite and limestone mountains that in the eastern part of the island reach an altitude of 7,870 feet. There are instead no active volcanoes on the Fijian islands whilst the Solomon Islands and Vanuatu are the setting for much of the region's seismic activity. In the Solomon Islands archipelago there are smoking craters on the islands of Tinakula, Savo, Simbo and Vella Lavella and below the sea to the south of New Georgia. There is another submarine volcano spewing magma in the Vanuatu archipelago near the island of Tongoa and terrestrial craters on Gaua, Ambrym and Lopevi. Initially formed from the magma erupting from the craters, the islands of Vanuatu have been consolidated by limestone platforms created by tectonic uplifting. The principal island of the New Caledonia archipelago, Grande Terre, also has a complex geology in which volcanic, sedimentary and metamorphic rocks are superimposed. New Caledonia's great environmental attraction is, however, its coral reef. This is the second largest such marine ecosystem in the world after the Australian Great Barrier Reef, with a length of 994 miles and a lagoon area of 8,900 square miles with an average depth of 66 feet. The reef is home to 1,500 species of fish which swim among the 350 varieties of coral and 20,000 species of invertebrates.

MELANESIA: BLACK ISLANDS, JUNGLES AND VOLCANOES

118 top Grande Terre, the main island of New Caledonia, is literally engulfed by luxuriant vegetation. The geology of the island is very complex with various strata having been identified and rocks of volcanic origin alternating with sedimentary deposits and metamorphic rocks.

118 bottom The Lau archipelago, situated in the easternmost waters of Fiji, is composed of 57 islands of volcanic and coralline origins. Its inhabitants have strong Polynesian ties, so much so that up until the mid-nineteenth century the area was claimed by both Fiji and Tonga.

118-119 The Ile des Pins is the most spectacular island in the New Caledonia archipelago, ringed by pure white sands and protected by a coral reef enclosing a turquoise lagoon populated by hundreds of varieties of tropical fish.

119 bottom New Guinea is traversed by a mountain range covering half the territory and culminating in the 15,400-foot peak of Mount Wilhelm. The relief features stretch for over 1,240 miles along the east-west axis and give rise to broad, deep valleys.

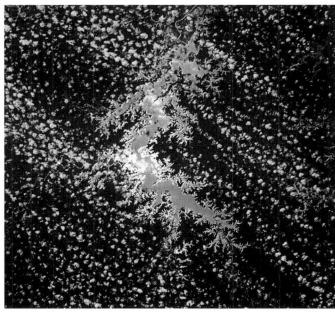

120-121 Cape Va's in Irian Jaya (the Indonesian part of New Guinea) extends towards Australia into the Arafura Sea. This photo, taken by a NASA satellite, shows a swampy region with an extremely low population density and divided by the River Digul.

121 top The eruption of the volcano Rabaul in New Guinea on the 19th of September, 1994, forced 50,000 people out of their homes and produced a column of smoke 59,000 feet high in the atmosphere, as can be seen in this photo taken by the American astronauts aboard the NASA space shuttle Discovery.

121 center This extraordinary image of Lake Murray in New Guinea was taken by a NASA satellite exploiting the double effect of polarization and double reverberation. The lake is situated between the Rivers Fly and Strickland which traverse a flood plain.

121 bottom This photo, taken by a NASA satellite, shows New Guinea, a mountainous island covered with rain-forests, shrouded in mist and inhabited by a thousand primitive tribes of black peoples, Papuans and Pygmies.

122 top The Solomon Islands form the most primitive and neglected archipelago in the Pacific. At the basis of the social structure is the clan, an extended family of up to 200 members whose genealogy, handed down via the oral tradition, can be traced as far back as ten generations.

122-123 The Nekoiar Festival on the island of Tanna (Vanuatu) features the toka, a ceremonial dance that accompanies the circumcision of boys who have reached the age of puberty. The event is also celebrated with the slaughtering of a large number of pigs.

obtained), the first Melanesian ethnographic model was established. Having settled, a number of tribes tied via marriage and alliances, sealed by ritual and commercial exchanges. The over one thousand ethnic groups still present today in New Guinea are linked by the absence of both authoritarian structures and the transmission of power via inheritance. The villages are led by the "big man" who has reached his position of power on merit rather than through descent.

While the Vedda Indians have prevailed in the Negroid features of the Melanesians, migrations from South-east China lie behind the diverse languages spoken in the region. Idioms that, combined with many English words introduced by the colonists in the mid-nineteenth century, gave rise to *pidgin*, a language widely spoken in Papua New Guinea, the Solomon Islands and Vanuatu, that has become the means whereby inhabitants of the various archipelagos communicate amongst themselves and with their western interlocutors.

The other ethnic group that reached New Guinea was that of the Murray or Ainoid group, this last name

The Melanesians, the first inhabitants of the Pacific

According to the latest research the first Melanesian island to be inhabited was New Guinea, colonized 50,000 years ago by hunter-gatherer tribes from Southeast Asia. They initially reached the island via the tongue of land that still linked it to the Indonesian archipelago and the Malay peninsula. Later, primitive rafts allowed them to shuttle from one Indonesian island to the next without ever losing sight of land. There were two clearly distinct peoples. The Vedda from western India, the oldest ethnic group in Asia, were semi-nomadic cave dwellers, small in stature with snub noses, receding chins, very dark skin, fleshy lips and wavy or curly hair. They settled on the northern and southern coasts of New Guinea and on the islands and coasts of the Gulf of Carpantaria (north-east Australia). These origins link the Melanesians with the Dravidian peoples of India, the dominant stock of the subcontinent prior to the arrival of the Indo-Arians, today restricted to the Tamil and Malay groups living in the south of the country. Following this migration black peoples settled in the highlands of New Guinea and spread to Australia, then still joined to New Guinea by the shallows and banks of sand that created a natural bridge with Cape York Peninsula. The peoples of New Guinea in fact belong to the same stock as the Australian Aboriginals, in spite of the fact that due to diverse environmental conditions they have developed very different customs and lifestyles. For at least 20,000 years the inhabitants of New Guinea led a typically nomadic hunter-gatherer existence, living in small tribes composed of just a few families who continuously wandered the territory in order to follow herds of wild pigs or reach areas rich in fruits. Settlement in small villages in the highlands of the interior and on the coast coincided with the advent of agriculture. With the rearing of pigs combined in the mountains with the cultivation of sweet potatoes and on the plains by sago (a palm from which edible flour was

123 top The island of Beqa in the Fijian archipelago, is famous for its fire walkers. Legend has it that thanks to an ancestor who spared the life of an eel during a fishing trip, the males of the Sawau tribe have the ability to walk on incandescent rocks.

123 bottom Many inhabitants of New Caledonia are the result of the inter-racial contacts between the French colonists and the original Melanesian population. The French occupied the archipelago in 1853 and transformed it into a penal colony. Today it is still a French overseas territory.

deriving from their physical relationship with the Ainu race of Japan. It was out of the crossing of these two peoples that the Melanesian native was born with dark skin, fuzzy or curly hair, Oriental eyes protected by prominent brows, a flattened nose, large and at times pendulous lips and a bodily stature similar to or smaller than that of Europeans but much smaller than that of the Maoris. When the sea level rose at the end of the last Ice Age, cutting the natural land bridges, the peoples of New Guinea remained trapped on the island and locked in the Stone Age.

Not until around 4000 BC, after having learned how to build outrigger canoes and to govern them amidst the violent ocean waves, did the inhabitants of New Guinea undertake new migrations and colonize the Trobiand Islands and the Bismarck archipelago (New Britain, New Ireland and a further 200 minor islands) and from there a number of Micronesian islands. From Micronesia they were forced by demographic pressure towards the Solomon Islands, Vanuatu, New Caledonia and Fiji

which were colonized over the course of a number of centuries.

In the Fijian islands the facial features and cultural characteristics of the Melanesians were mixed with those of the Polynesians. The Fijians have lighter skin and softer features than the other Melanesians and their cultural traditions have more in common with those of Tonga and Samoa than those of the Solomon Islands or New Guinea. Apart from Fiji, the rest of the Melanesian archipelagos retain ethnic and cultural affinities. There are no tribal chieftains (except in New Caledonia), councils of elders or centralized structures. Melanesian society is much more primitive than that in Polynesia, with women being the weak links, not to say victims. On many islands wives are bought by their husbands, considered to be inferior beings, frequently subjected to violence and in some ethnic groups—such as those of the highlands of New Guinea—are expected to nurse piglets as well as their own children.

The scarcity of archaeological relics—the oldest are Lapita ceramics dating from 1500 BC—and the continual

124 top left This man belongs to the ethnic group known as the Fore, inhabitants of New Guinea well known to western physicians due to their custom of eating the brains of their dead. This macabre practice led to the development of the disease kuru, *known in the West as spongiform encephalitis.*

124-125 The Dani were discovered on the banks of the River Baliem in the north of Irian Jaya by an expedition organized by the New York Museum of Natural History in 1938. They lived naked raising pigs that were frequently wet-nursed by the women of the tribe.

124 bottom This portrait of a Papuan native illustrates the physical differences compared with the other ethnic groups of New Guinea.

125 top The Pygmies of New Guinea descend from the first Melanesian Black peoples who emigrated to the island. Their stature is a consequence of their adaptation to unfavourable environmental conditions. The man in the photo is portrayed in the forests beyond the River Famek in Irian Jaya.

125 bottom Among the numerous macabre practices common to many of the ethnic groups living in the mountains of New Guinea, is the kind of living cemetery of the Fore people of Papua New Guinea, with the deceased covered with mud and set in seated poses on stages.

revision of history by way of the oral tradition leave few certainties with regards to the remote past of Melanesia and that of Oceania as a whole. Some anthropologists claim, for example, that the Solomon Islands were populated around 30,000 years ago. Such a dating would radically modify the history of oceanic navigation, unless one accepts the rather weak hypothesis that it was possible to reach the Solomon Islands from New Guinea by way of the Bismarck archipelago, floating from one island to the next on crude bamboo rafts with no sails. What is certain is that all the Melanesian peoples shared spiritualist rituals and the practice of cannibalism for which there were various motivations. Above all, enemies killed in battle were eaten to acquire their spiritual power. However, many tribes in New Guinea considered the men of other ethnic groups as mere game to be hunted and eaten as if they were wild pigs. In Fiji, the preparation of the "long pig" (as human flesh was called) took on gastronomic overtones with recipes for its cooking and rituals for its consumption, and the Fijians, in contrast with the other Pacific islanders, are actually proud of their cannibalistic past.

126 The cassowary (Casuarius casuarius) is a flightless bird present in both New Guinea and the forests of northern Queensland (Australia). Almost 71 inches tall, it has black plumage, a form of crest on its head and a blue throat from which hang long red wattles.

127 top The spotted cuscus (Spilocuscus maculatus) is one of the many marsupials found in New Guinea. It is an arboreal animal with nocturnal habits. It moves easily through the branches of trees thanks to robust curving claws and a prehensile tail slightly shorter than its body.

127 bottom left This photo, taken on the island of Biak, shows a crowned dove, one of the most spectacular of the hundreds of birds identified in Irian Jaya, the western region of New Guinea under the control of Indonesia since 1963.

127 bottom right This species of arboreal kangaroo (Dendrogagus ursinus) was photographed in the north-western mountains of Irian Jaya. The majority of the mammals recorded in New Guineas are marsupials. The placentates are restricted to bats and a number of rodents.

128 top *The mountainous region immediately inland from the Coral Coast in the south of Viti Levu, is one of the most fertile in Fiji. It is traversed by rivers such as the Sigatoka which runs through the valley of the same name that is also known as the "salad bowl" because of the intensive cultivation of leaf vegetables.*

128-129 *Nukubati is an island with beautiful white beaches and an interior covered with coconut plantations. This is the only island equipped for tourism off the north coast of Vanua Levu, a seaboard generally inaccessible because of the dense mangroves.*

Fiji: smiling racial blend

perfumed with curry

Located on the dividing line between Melanesia—to which it belongs—and Polynesia, the Fijian archipelago is composed of 330 islands (of which only 106 are inhabited) with a total surface area of 7,053 square miles and scattered across a stretch of ocean as large as France and Great Britain combined. The Fijian islands are for the most part of volcanic origin—although there are no active craters—except for a number of sandy atolls that have formed close to the coral reefs of the Lau and Mamanuca archipelagos. Crossed by the 180th meridian, the International Date Line, the Fiji archipelago features four main, mountainous islands, Viti Levu, Vanua Levu, Kadavu and Taveuni, with forests, three-quarters of them virgin rain forests, covering 60% of the territory. The Fijian islands are distinguished from the other oceanic archipelagos by their botanical variety: over 3,000 plant species have been catalogued, a third of which are endemic, including one thousand flowering plants. From the point of view of fauna, they are instead similar to the other islands with native mammals restricted to a species of rat and two bats and a total of seven different species of amphibians and reptiles. Here too the animal world is dominated by the birds, with 126 different species having been recorded. The principal and largest island is Viti Levu, cut in two by a range of mountains that acts as a dividing line between the damp eastern side covered with forest vegetation, and the dry west coast where large sugarcane plantations are to be found. This form of agriculture has over the last century radically altered Fiji, from a racial point of view as well as that of landscape. Initially inhabited by Polynesians—the islands were once one of the centers of the Lapita civilization—around 500 BC the Fijian archipelago was invaded by Negro peoples from New Guinea. There was a cruel battle between cannibalistic tribes: archaeological evidence and legends passed on orally demonstrate that eating one's enemies was common practice. William Bligh, the captain of the *Bounty* who passed through the archipelago in a small boat in 1789 after the famous mutiny, called them the "Cannibal Islands." In many Fijians the typical Melanesian facial features are softened by Maori influence, while various customs—from *tapa*, a fabric made from the bark of a species of mulberry, to *kava*, a ritual drink with narcotic effects—link them to Polynesia. Early in the nineteenth century, when the first Europeans landed in the islands, the Fijians were living in villages composed of clans led by an hereditary chieftain (another link with Polynesia) and were frequently involved in tribal disputes. In 1840, the chieftain Cakobau managed to gain ascendency over his rivals and claimed the title of King of Fiji. His was not a happy reign as problems of a civil and military nature arose with the United States following a dubious commercial transaction. The King of Tonga took advantage of further tribal conflicts on Viti Levu to extend his power over the Lau Islands (where still today the population is Polynesian), Taveuni and part of Vanua Levu. The end of Fijian autonomy was, however, determined by the growing British interest in the tropical crops of cotton and sugarcane. Not even the conversion to Christianity put an end to the tribal warfare, and thus in 1874 Cakobau, tired of the situation, the island ceded power to the British. Incapable of making the islanders work in the plantations, the colonists imported labor from India. As a consequence, half of the Fijian Islands' present-day population (780,000 inhabitants) are Indian and the co-existence is far from peaceful. After the

130 top The Lau archipelago is in environmental terms the best preserved of the Fijian group. Despite the paradisical scenery of its islands, tourism has yet to develop to any great degree. One of the atolls was acquired in the 1970s by Raymond Burr, the actor famous for playing Perry Mason.

130 center Turtle Island is the best known of the Yasawa Group, an archipelago composed of 16 volcanic islands situated to the north-west of Viti Levu. Their scenery, some of the most spectacular in the Pacific, features white beaches overlooked by rugged mountain peaks and enclosed within blue lagoons.

130 bottom The Fijian Mamanuca archipelago is composed of 13 atolls situated to the west of Viti Levu. The interior of the coralline islands is cloaked in luxuriant tropical forests, rimmed by beaches of fine white sand that slope into the ocean towards the coral reef.

archipelago was granted independence in 1970, the Indians felt themselves to be second class citizens. Despite the fact that they represent the professional, intellectual and commercial classes, they are unable to buy land which the Native Land Trust Board inalienably assigns to the tribal communities. They also have restricted political rights: the Labor victory backed by the Indians was overturned in 1987 by a nationalist coup d'état that excluded them from the most important state posts and guaranteed a majority of seats in parliament for the natives. In spite of these ethnic problems, the Fijians are one the Pacific's friendliest peoples, ever ready to burst into riotous laughter. This factor, together with the beauty of the landscape, has transformed the Fijian Islands into one of the region's principal tourist destinations. Following the urbanization of the areas of Nadi (the site of the international airport) and Suva (the capital) by the British, the influx of foreign capital has permitted the development of a hotel industry supported by an efficient network of services, with tourism now being the island's major source of income. This is followed by sugar production and manufacturing industries attracted by low labor costs. The tourists themselves are attracted by some of the most spectacular scenery in the Pacific, such as the Yasawa archipelago, sixteen islands with volcanic peaks dropping down to endless beaches of white sand fringed with coconut palms. Together with the nearby Mamanuca atolls, the Yasawas house exclusive resorts and are visited by numerous cruise ships. Between Taveuni and the south-east coast of Vanua Levu, there are some of the ocean's richest sea-beds, for the exploration of which Jean-Michel Cousteau, the son of the French oceanographer Jacques-Yves, has opened an eco-compatible diving resort.

131 Varua Balavu is the second largest island in the Lau archipelago (Fiji). Its extremely complex coastline forms the shape of a sea-shores. It is a rock platform of volcanic origins, although its northernmost tip is a coral formation.

132-133 The lagoon of Turtle Island in the Yasawa Group (Fiji) was the natural setting for the film "The Blue Lagoon" and its remake. The original version from 1948 starred Jean Simmons and Ed Huston, while the second from 1980 featured Brooke Shields and Chris Atkins.

132 bottom Ovalu, a volcanic island in the Lomainviti archipelago, houses Levuka, the former capital of Fiji. The city was established in 1830 as a whaling port and, following the opening of a British consulate, became the fulcrum of the kingdom of Cakobau, the last king of Fiji.

133 top Among the native peoples of Fiji, Melanesian customs and physical characteristics are mixed with those of the Polynesians. The archipelago was, in fact, initially inhabited by Maoris and later invaded by Blacks from New Guinea.

133 bottom In Fiji students wear a uniform that differs in form and color according to the school they attend, a relic of British colonialism, as are the fifty percent of the population of Indian origin, introduced by the British to cultivate sugarcane.

New Guinea: the wild

With three-quarters of its territory covered with rain-forests shrouded in cloud and inhabited by a thousand primitive tribes of black people, Papuans and Pygmies, at the dawn of the new millennium New Guinea remains one of the planet's most primitive, most mysterious and wildest places. During the 1970s, the last community of cave-dwellers was discovered in the caverns of Karawari. New Guinea represents the frontier between the Indian and Pacific Oceans and between Asia and Oceania, and is the world's second largest island after Greenland with a surface area of 303,000 square miles (geographers consider Australia to be a continent rather than an island). It has a geographical and cultural homogeneity, but among the mountains and the jungles of its interior a political border follows the 141st meridian, dividing it into two states of virtually identical size. To the west is Irian Jaya, controlled by Indonesia, while to the east is the independent state of Papua New Guinea. An imposing mountain range runs for almost 1,250 miles along the east-west axis of the island, covering half of the territory and culminating in the 15,396-foot high Mount Wilhelm. This backbone is furrowed by deep, broad valleys located at altitudes of between 4,900 and 9,850 feet above sea level, cloaked in dripping jungle and incised by powerful rivers fed by one of the earth's wettest climates (the interior receives an average annual rainfall of 196 inches). The Sepik river is 700 miles long and crosses much of the north-western region of Papua New Guinea. The entire island is modelled by relief features, the principal mountain range running southwards with irregular formations characterized by hundreds of valleys and rivers contributing to the formation of flood plains and endless swamps such as the Meervlakte or "Plain of Lakes," a flat swamp region in the south of Irian Jaya at the confluence of the Tariku and Teritatu rivers in the Mamberamo basin.

For millennia, such rugged and impenetrable terrain presented an obstacle to communication between the various ethnic groups and encouraged the development of a vast number of languages and cultures. In the two states into which the island is divided today, over one thousand languages and dialects of the Papuan and Austronesian stocks are spoken. 240 idioms are spoken in Irian Jaya and 769 in Papua New Guinea where the various groups communicate with each other in *pidgin*, a language in which English and native terms are used. Even though the total population of Irian Jaya and Papua New Guinea combined is little over 6 million, the island presents one of the world's most complex ethnic and linguistic profiles. Almost all of the tribes of New Guinea still live in primitive and extremely poor societies, inhabiting villages located in the highlands or on the banks of navigable rivers. They are organized in patrilineal clans with descent passing through the paternal line and celebrate exogamous marriages, that is to say with members of other groups. Their economy is based on the cultivation of sweet potatoes and other tubers and the raising of pigs. Religion revolves around spiritualism, magic, the cult of the dead and communication with the spirits. Mediumistic ceremonies and cruel initiatory rites are overseen by all-powerful shamans. The atmosphere of these rituals owes much to the traditional masks and idols in painted wood produced by many of the ethnic groups.

Among the most well known and most populous tribes are the native Papuans, who live on the navigable rivers in the south of Papua New Guinea and are distinguished from the coastal Melanesians by their lighter skin and the shape of their noses, convex in the case of the first and broad or snubbed in the second. The Papuans are related to the forest dwelling pygmies from the banks of the River Famek. Among the first of the highlands tribes to come into contact with the westerners was that of the Dani. In 1938, an expedition organized by the New York Museum of Natural History discovered a number of villages along the banks of the Baliem river in the north of Irian Jaya. Still part of the Stone Age, the Dani lived completely naked, raising pigs that were frequently wet-nursed by the women of the tribe. The men wore penis sheaths, considered to be symbols of virility, capable of protecting the organ from malign influences. This sexual ornament is still today used by the males of many ethnic groups, such as the Yali who, like the Dani, the Asmat and the

134-135 The majority of the tribes of New Guinea live in primitive villages in the highlands on the banks of navigable rivers. Their economy is based on the cultivation of sweet potatoes and other tubers and raising of pigs.

135 top The men living in the coastal villages of Papua New Guinea (the eastern half of the island) take to the sea, above all to fish, in outrigger canoes, a type of boat found among all the peoples of the Pacific Ocean.

crossroads of oceanic man

Papuans, also wear animal bones through their noses.

The first Europeans to land on the island were the sixteenth century Portuguese and Spanish navigators, including Yñigo Ortiz de Retes, who named it New Guinea as its dense forests and black natives reminded him of Guinea in Africa. Malaria, swamps, a torrid climate, impenetrable jungle and bellicose tribes of cannibals and head-hunters kept the Europeans away from the island for centuries. In 1623, the Dutchman Jan Carstenz climbed the mountains of present-day Irian Jaya and encountered the Asmat, but back in Europe his accounts were disregarded. For thousands of years the westernmost tip of New Guinea had relationships with the Macassan peoples of Sulawesi and with various Indonesian sultanates, and it was thus natural for the Dutch to incorporate the territory within their East Indies empire in 1828. The Dutch presence was, however, restricted to the coastal regions. The same was also true of the Germans, who in 1884, settled on the north-east coast and the English, who colonized the south-eastern seaboard. In the second half of the nineteenth century, the Italian naturalist Luigi D'Albertis explored the Arfak mountains and the Fly river during the course of two separate expeditions. In 1906, the British colony passed to Australia which, following the First World War, also took control of the German possessions. The interior, however, remained unexplored until once again gold fever was responsible for stimulating men's sense of adventure. In 1930, in search of gold, the Australians Mick Dwyer and Mick Lehay ventured into the wild valleys of the Chimbu inhabited by Stone Age tribes. During the Second World War, New Guinea was invaded by the Japanese and became the theater of violent battles. Following the Dutch decolonization, the western part of the island came under the control of

Indonesia in 1963 and was eventually renamed Irian Jaya. Irian is the acronym of the Ikut Republik Indonesia Anti-Nederland (with the Indonesian Republic against the Netherlands), whilst Jaya means "victorious," a name reflecting the anti-colonial nature of the state's creation. This is ironic in that the peoples of Irian Jaya have nothing in common with Indonesia and for decades its army has had to deal with the guerrilla tactics of the Free Papua Movement (Organisasi Papua Merdeka). Following the annexation of the island, the government in Jakarta encouraged immigration from other over-crowded parts of Indonesia, distributing land to the new colonists. Today at least 700,000 Javanese live in Irian Jaya, forming above all the bureaucratic apparatus, whilst trade is in the hands of the Chinese. For some years, work has been in progress on the construction of the Trans-Irian Highway, an 497-mile road that will cross the Maoke and Wanema mountains, the homeland of the Dani, and link the capital Jayapura with the city of Merauke on the north and south coasts respectively.

In 1975, Papua New Guinea was granted independence from Australia, which nonetheless continues to offer its

cooperation and aid in the extraction of prime materials. The country, with around four and half million inhabitants, is still very underdeveloped: there is a lack of railway links and roads and the economy is based on subsistence agriculture in villages with no services. In contrast with Irian Jaya, Papua New Guinea has instead developed a tourist industry based on the underwater marvels of the Coral Sea off the south coast, as well as on the appeal of its landscape and folklore. The capital, Port Moresby, takes its name from the first European to land there in 1873, and is located on the south-east coast. It is composed of an agglomeration of villages spreading over a hilly promontory. There is a colorful market in the Koki district and a cultural center with huts and costumes from various tribes in that of Konedobu. The 600 tropical islands, for the most part of volcanic origins, scattered across the Pacific to the north-east of the main island are also part of Papua New Guinea. Most of them fall within the Bismarck archipelago, itself composed of the island groups of New Britain, New Ireland, Manus, Bougainville and another 200 minor islands that together cover 22,983 square miles and a total population of around 450,000 inhabitants. The island of

140-141 The Yali people first came into contact with white men in 1945, when an American reconnaissance plane crashed in the Jaxolè valley. For the tribe this was a sign of the destabilization of the cosmic order, of the equilibrium between the living and the dead.

140 bottom The earliest research into the customs of the Yali people was conducted by the anthropologist Kalus Friedrich Kock, who arrived in Yalimo (the country of the Yali) in 1964. The tribe still practices cannibalism as a form of vendetta, the last episodes being recorded in 1968.

Bougainville (which takes its name from the French explorer who discovered it in 1768), the easternmost of the archipelago, belongs politically to Papua New Guinea but shares the language, traditions and customs of the Solomon Islands. Due to its geographical and cultural ties with the Melanesian archipelago-state, Bougainville is also known as the Northern Solomons. The unusual ethnic make-up of its population has, over the last decade, stimulated a separatist movement that has disturbed the island's way of life with numerous military actions. The inhabitants of the Trobriand Islands, located off the eastern tail of Papua New Guinea, are also clearly distinguished from the other peoples of New Guinea. They form an unusual Melanesian ethnic group (with Polynesian influences) of fishermen and farmers that exchange their respective food surpluses during encounters that have ceremonial as well as economic foundations. Society in the Trobriand Islands is based around matrilineal clans (with descent passing through the maternal line) and is still today the most sexually permissive in the Pacific with widespread promiscuity, in part because of the belief that children are conceived not by the men but by the spirit of the island. Early in the twentieth century, this permissiveness, together with the natural beauty of the population and the magical landscape, transformed the Trobriands into the mythical paradise of the South Seas. A romantic exaggeration stimulated by the book *Argonauts of the Western Pacific*, by the Polish geographer Bronislaw Malinowski—the first westerner to visit the archipelago—and the consequent interest aroused among anthropologists who transformed the native islanders into one of the most intensively studied ethnic groups on earth.

141 bottom A Yali village in the Seng can be seen in this photo. The members of this ethnic group number around 30,000 and live in the mountains to the east of the Baliem valley where they construct their settlements on plateaus at altitudes of up to 7,200 feet.

141 top The Yali children spend most of their time with the women and contacts with the adult men are rare. According to the ethnologists, this separation is the fruit of a violent society that tends to be aggressive partly as a result of the continual tribal warfare.

141 center The Yali live in the highlands of New Guinea, raise pigs and cultivate sugarcane, sweet potatoes, yam (a tuber rich in starch) and taro (a plant whose leaves and succulent roots, a source of vitamins and natural salts, are eaten).

142 top This Korowai man is wearing a large ring through his nose. The custom of piercing the nostrils with metal rings, animal bones, sticks or rods (placed horizontally or vertically) is common to almost all the ethnic groups of New Guinea.

142-143 This group of men is constructing a house in the upper branches of a tree. Some of the last tree-dwelling tribes live in southern Irian Jaya, on the course of the Brazza, Pulau Pulau and Dàiram Kabùr rivers and some tributaries of the Dughul.

143 bottom left The homes of the Korowai people (Irian Jaya) are built on stilts, tree trunks or branches at heights of up to around 66 feet from the ground. The tree dwellings are considered necessary by a tribe that lives in a state of perpetual war.

143 bottom right The forest provides the raw materials for the Citak, Kombai and Korowai peoples to build their homes at the tops of the trees. The huts are frequently constructed a number of miles from one another, but occasionally groups of up to four homes may be found.

142 bottom The homes of the Korowai in the tops of the trees are easily defended. This ethnic group from Irian Jaya is one of the most aggressive in New Guinea and lives in constant conflict with its neighbors and it is thought that the group still practices cannibalism.

144 top left Following the veto on tribal warfare imposed by the Indonesians in 1963, the Dani have become the most tranquil of the ethnic groups in Irian Jaya, have permanent relationships with the authorities and missionaries, attend schools and each year welcome around a thousand tourists.

144 bottom The Dani men practice polygamy. For them, as for many other ethnic groups in New Guinea, the valor of a man is proportional to the number of women and pigs he possesses.

145 This bellicose image evokes the traditions of the Dani people, an ethnic group of warriors who fought with bows, arrows and long spears. The conflicts were accompanied by ritual ceremonies as complex as they were cruel. Today tribal warfare is sporadic.

144 top right The Dani men, like those of many other ethnic groups of New Guinea, wear a holim, a penis sheath made from a dried gourd and supported by a cord tied around the waist. The sheath is a symbol of virility and an amulet protecting the genitals.

144 center This photo shows a group of Dani cooking food on a bed of red-hot stones. The economy of this ethnic group is based on the raising of pigs and the cultivation of sweet potatoes, which represent 90% of their diet.

146-147 For the Asmat people (Irian Jaya), the animal bones worn through the nose are mourning custom. Asmat means "men of the trees." According to their philosophy, man is the tree of life with the body being the trunk, the arms the branches and the legs the roots.

146 bottom These members of the Fore tribe, an ethnic group from Papua New Guinea are performing a magical ritual. The masks are used by the majority of the island's tribes on the occasion of ceremonies based on spiritualism, the cult of the dead and communication with the spirits.

147 top The Papuans, the ethnic group that lends its name to the independent state of Papua New Guinea, live along the navigable rivers of the south-west regions of the island. They are distinguished from the Melanesians by their lighter skin and snub noses.

147 bottom The coastal regions of Papua New Guinea are inhabited by Melanesian peoples who are clearly distinguished from the Papuans by their very dark skin and convex noses. It was this ethnic group that colonized the archipelagos of Melanesia.

Vanuatu is one of Oceania's most traditional archipelagos. Having left Port Vila, the cosmopolitan modern capital inhabited by Europeans, Chinese and Vietnamese and the location of the international airport and almost all the country's modern facilities, one plunges into a prehistory of jungles and villages inhabited by men wearing nothing but penis sheaths. The archipelago is composed of 82 islands (67 of which are inhabited) distributed along a longitudinal axis stretching 807 miles. In actual fact, the twelve principal mountainous islands of volcanic origin with plains restricted to the coastal belts account for almost all of the 5,700 square miles of the national territory. Initially formed from the magma flowing from the craters, the islands have been consolidated by limestone platforms created as a result of

Vanuatu: the enchanted islands of Bungee Jumping

tectonic lifting. Situated on the Ring of Fire, where the Pacific plate slips beneath the Indo-Australian plate, Vanuatu is characterized by active volcanoes; a submarine crater near the island of Tongoa and the three terrestrial cones of Gaua, Ambrym and Lopevi. This last erupted on a number of occasions in the 1970s. The volcanoes contribute to a rugged landscape strewn with caverns, waterfalls, geysers and hot springs. The meeting of the two plates has also created the New Hebrides Trench, a marine abyss over 26,200 feet deep. The hot, wet climate favours the growth of the dense vegetation which covers three-quarters of the territory. The principal botanical curiosity is a variety of giant banyan, the *Ficus bengalensis*, with extremely extensive roots that can grow to heights of almost a hundred feet. It is believed that the archipelago was peopled around 3000 BC, although the earliest archaeological relics date from almost 2,000 years later. 95% of the population of 190,000 people are Melanesians. A Polynesian minority lives on the islands of Futuna, Emae and Ambae and in a number of villages on Efate. 105 native dialects are spoken, but 60% of the population are able to express themselves in *pidgin*. Subsistence agriculture (taro, manioc and sweet potatoes) provides food for four-fifths of the population and is the mainstay of a primitive economy in which imports outstrip exports five-fold and a precarious balance is maintained thanks only to international aid. Vanuatu has the unenviable record in Oceania for infant mortality, illiteracy and demographic expansion, with half of the inhabitants under fifteen years of age. In the 1990s, there has been a considerable increase in tourism, encouraged by the continual search for new destinations.

The first European to reach Vanuatu was the Spaniard Pedro Fernando de Quiros in 1605, followed in 1768 by Bougainville. But it was James Cook who surveyed the islands

in 1774 and named them the New Hebrides after the Scottish archipelago. Cloaked as it was in jungles and inhabited by aggressive cannibals who regulated relationships between villages with gifts of pigs and exchanges of wives, the islands failed to attract the interest of the European powers. Today, the majority of the inhabitants are Christians, but John Williams, the first missionary to land in Vanuatu, was killed and eaten on the island of Erromanga. Only in the second half of the nineteenth century did French and British colonists establish plantations of cotton, bananas, coconut palms, coffee and cocoa on diverse islands. It was Germany's interest in the region that persuaded London and Paris to transform the New Hebrides into a shared Anglo-French colony. An important American base during the Second World War with 100,000 marines stationed on the island of Espiritu Santo, the archipelago was granted independence in 1980 with the name Vanuatu, meaning "Eternal Life," a republic based on Melanesian customs. Along with dances, large, imaginative masks, arrows decorated with spectacular feathers, sculptures with human or animal features and drums so tall and so highly decorated as to resemble totems (they are carved from tree trunks), Vanuatu's most famous tradition is that of the *naghol* from Pentecost Island. A leap into the void with the ankles secured by a liana, the ritual from which bungee jumping derives, an extreme sport now practiced throughout the world. In effect, *naghol* means "leap into the void" and this is one of the most spectacular of the Oceanic ceremonies, a test of courage for adolescent males and a propitiatory ritual on the occasion of the harvesting of yams, the tubers that represent the island's principal food resource. When the first sprouts appear in April, the natives use trunks and branches bound with lianas to build a hundred-foot-high tower, an enterprise that occupies the entire village for about a month. On the day of the *naghol*, the villagers congregate at the foot of the tower where they dance accompanied by a monotonous chant as they await the moment of truth. Each jump, which may be made by children as young as ten, is acclaimed with cries and prolonged applause. According to a Pentecost Island legend, the *naghol* derives from the story of Tamalié, an islander who always followed his unfaithful wife. One day the woman climbed the highest tree on the island. The man followed her to the top but just before he caught her she dived into the void—after having tied her ankles with robust lianas. The jealous husband imitated her leap, but having failed to secure himself with lianas, he plunged to his death.

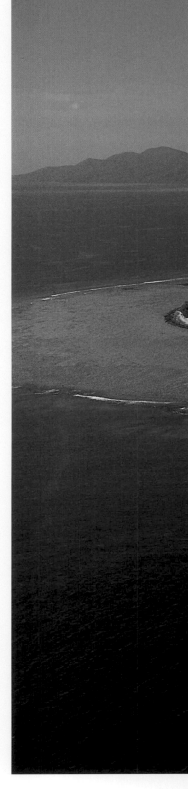

148 top The Yasur volcano in the island of Tanna, one of the southernmost of the Vanuatu archipelago, is still active. Much of the interior of the island is occupied by coffee plantations whilst the coastline is rimmed with long beaches of black sand.

148 bottom Tanna is the island in the Vanuatu archipelago with the most deeply-rooted tribal traditions. Marriage and the circumcision of boys who have reached the age of puberty are accompanied by dancing. The majority of the ceremonies such as the famous Nekoviar Festival take place in July and August.

148-149 This photo depicts Lamen Island, an atoll surrounded by a coral reef. In the background can be seen the three volcanic islands of Epi, Lopevi and Paama. The Vanuatu archipelago is composed of 82 islands, 67 of which are inhabited, divided into 3 groups.

149 top For the islanders who inhabit Pentecost in the Vanuatu archipelago, the naghol is both a test of courage and a propitiatory ritual associated with the agricultural cycles. During the ceremony, the "athletes" jump into the void with their ankles secured by robust lianas that interrupt their fall a couple of inches from the ground. The ceremony is the origin of bungee jumping, an extreme sport now practiced throughout the world.

150 top The Solomon Islands were peopled around 4,000 years ago by Melanesian farmers speaking an Austronesian language. Mountainous and inhabited by aggressive peoples who practiced war dances and cruel initiation ceremonies, this was one of the most difficult archipelagos to colonize.

150-151 The mountainous Guadalcanal, the largest of the Solomon Islands, is of volcanic origins and is covered with rain-forests. The highest peak is that of Mount Popomanatseu at 7,646 feet. In the mid-nineteenth century, Guadalcanal became the principal British base in this area of Melanesia.

151 top Some of the most suggestive rituals of the Solomon Islands are performed on the island of Malaita, dances associated with the land and the sea such as the offering of food to the sharks (in which the natives believe that spirits of their ancestors are reincarnated) in the Langa Langa lagoon.

151 bottom The interior of the Solomon Islands is covered with rugged relief features of volcanic origin. The vast majority of the archipelago's population live in the flat coastal regions that are stabilized by mangroves and coconut palms and protected by coral reefs.

Solomon Islands:

Solomon Islands also include myriad atolls such as Rennell, one of the best examples of an elevated calcareous island and as such included in UNESCO's World Heritage List.

Although some studies claim that the islands were peopled around 30,000 years ago by hunter-gathers from New Guinea, a more reliable theory is that Melanesian cultivators speaking an Austronesian language migrated here around 2,000 BC. Carbon 14 testing has, in fact, dated stone tools back 4,000 years while the remains of homes date from 1,300 BC. On the island of Santa Cruz, excavations have brought to light Lapita ceramics—from the proto-Polynesian civilization—that came from New Caledonia around 3,000 years ago.

Having established bases on the island of Guadalcanal, the British used the Solomon Islands as a source of forced labor. Between 1870 and 1910 they deported 30,000 natives to

the forgotten archipelago of the shark-men

The inhabitants of the Langa Langa lagoon on the island of Malaita belong to the sea like the fish to which they believe they are related. They live on artificial islands created with coral detritus, in houses with walls of bamboo and roofs of palm leaves. They believe that the spirits of their ancestors are reincarnated as the sharks to which they offer food after calling them with a gong struck in the water. This is the most suggestive of the customs of the Solomon Islands, the most primitive archipelago in the Pacific, ignored by modern tourism in spite of its wild beauty and one of the last corners of the world to fall under the political and religious control of the west. The Solomon Islands were discovered and named in 1568 by the Spaniard Alvaro Mendaña after he had reached them by following the Inca legend that spoke of treasure—similar to that of the biblical king—hidden on an archipelago 600 leagues west of Peru. In his attempt to colonize the islands Mendaña came into conflict with the natives and lost many of his men. During his second voyage he contracted malaria and died in 1595. On his maps, Mendaña located the Solomon Islands much further to the east than they are in reality, and thus for 200 years no other navigator managed to find them. They were eventually rediscovered in 1767 by the Englishman Philip Carteret, followed the year after by the Frenchman de Bougainville. The mountainous islands inhabited by aggressive peoples who practiced war dances and cruel initiation ceremonies and decorated the prows of their canoes with black-painted wooden idols proved difficult to colonize. A land of adventure surrounded by seas in which shipwrecks were frequent; a land all too often struck by hurricanes or earthquakes and where in order to reach the gold mines one had to run the risk of malaria. The Solomon Islands are, in fact, composed of 922 atolls and volcanic islands (347 of which inhabited) scattered across an area 1,118 miles broad on the latitudinal axis and 600 on the longitude, situated fair and square on the Ring of Fire. The islands of Tinakula, Savo, Simbo and Vella Lavella are dominated by active volcanoes and there is a submarine crater to the south of New Georgia. With a surface area of 10,630 square miles, the Solomon Islands archipelago is the second largest in the Pacific after that of New Guinea. The volcanic islands are corrugated by mountain ranges and cloaked in rainforests slashed by dramatic waterfalls. The highest peak is that of Popomanatseu (7,646 feet) on Guadalcanal, the largest island. The coastal regions, the most densely populated, are instead gently sloping, fixed by mangroves and coconut palms and rimmed by coral reefs. The

Queensland (Australia) and Fiji to work on the sugarcane plantations. After the German colonization of Bougainville and Buka—islands belonging to Papua New Guinea that have geographical, ethnic and linguistic ties with the Solomon Islands—in 1893 London declared the archipelago to be a British protectorate and established vast palm plantations for the production of copra. The Japanese invaded the Solomon Islands in 1942 and the archipelago became a theater of the war in the Pacific. President John Fitzgerald Kennedy and the writer James Michener fought on Guadacanal and the islands were the inspiration for Michener's book *Tales of the South Pacific*, for which he was awarded the Pulitzer Prise in 1948. In the post-war period, the British transferred the capital to Honiara, taking advantage of the facilities built by the Americans. Independence was granted to the archipelago in 1978. Today Honiara is a shabby city with little traffic, a second-rate market, the damp abandon of the tropics and nights fraught with criminal threats. It reflects the contemporary reality of the Solomon Islands, the forgotten corner of the Pacific. Only Guadalcanal and Malaita have a road network. There is no compulsory education and 85% of the population is illiterate. With a population of over 400,000 individuals, the majority under the age of 15, the state is the most prolific in Oceania. There is an abyss between the cities inhabited mainly by the Chinese and Europeans where *pidgin* is spoken and trade and profits of the mining industry permit a western lifestyle, and the villages in which four fifths of the population still live in traditional fashion and speak 120 different dialects. Their economy is based on fishing, livestock and subsistence agriculture while society revolves around the clan, an extended family of up to 200 members, the genealogy of which, handed down orally, stretches back up to ten generations.

New Caledonia:

The extraordinary luminosity enhancing the palette of colors painting its landscape has led to Grande Terre, the principal island of New Caledonia, being nicknamed the "Island of Light." Located just north of the Tropic of Capricorn, mid-way between Australia and Fiji, Grande Terre is a cigar-shaped island, 249 miles long and 31 wide, accounting for almost all of the archipelago's dry land. The island has a complex geology featuring volcanic, sedimentary and metamorphic rocks, a mountain range running its length, with peaks alternating with rugged green valleys incised by raging torrents, deep gorges and dramatic waterfalls. The northern and southern sides of the island are overlooked by two peaks of a similar height, Mount Panié (5,376 feet) and Mount Humboldt (5,400 feet). Much of the mountainous interior is covered with jungle vegetation, whilst the coastal landscape varies from the savannah alternating with mangroves of the west coast to the cliffs plunging to the lagoon in the north-east. The morphology and flora of Grande Terre have more in common with those of Australia than the other oceanic archipelagos. 3,250

botanical species have been cataloged, three-quarters of them endemic. The most common is the araucaria, a pine endemic to the Pacific and present here in 13 of the 16 classified varieties. The savannah areas are instead dominated by the *niaouli*, a tree similar to the eucalyptus with an important environmental role in that it survives the fires that raze the plains, guaranteeing reforestation. New Caledonia is also composed of the Ile des Pins and Belep, geological extensions of Grande Terre, the Loyalty Islands, composed of the Maré, Tiga, Lifou and Ouvéa atolls aligned around 62 miles east of Grande Terre, the micro-atolls of Huon, the limestone platform of Walpole with cliffs 230 feet high and the world's second largest coral reef after the Australian Great Barrier Reef, extending 994 miles and enclosing a lagoon of 8,878 square miles.

The earliest inhabitants of New Caledonia were the proto-Polynesian Lapita people. The ceramics that characterize the culture and date from 1,000 BC were discovered here for the first time. There are instead no factual grounds supporting the hypothesis based on the earthworks found on the Ile des Pins, claiming that man has inhabited these islands for 8,000 years. They were in fact constructed by an extinct species of giant bird related to the moa. The Lapita people were displaced by the black migrants from New Guinea who established the Melanesian Kanak culture based on the cultivation of tubers and wood sculpting. Clans composed of around fifty people lived in small villages and cultivated taro and above all yam on terraces created on the mountainsides. The land was owned collectively but administered by the first-born of the family that was the first to settle in the area. At the center of the village there would be a large hut with a conical roof in which the chief lived and spiritualist ceremonies were held in honor of dead ancestors. Diverse clans composed tribes that, due to the impenetrability of the terrain, had scarce contact with one another. The first European to land in New Caledonia was James Cook in 1774. He was followed by a number of missionaries and eventually the archipelago was annexed by the French in 1853 and transformed into a penal colony. Between 1864 and 1897, around 23,000 French prisoners were deported here, including thousands of Communards arrested after the insurrection of 1871, known as the Commune of Paris. The discovery of nickel (New Caledonia boasts 25% of world-wide deposits) encouraged the French to advance into the interior,

152-153 This aerial photo shows a bank of coral in New Caledonia, the French overseas territory that boasts the world's second longest barrier reef which extends for 994 miles and encloses a lagoon of 8,878 square miles.

153 top A mountain range runs the length of the island of Grande Terre with peaks alternating with brilliant green rugged valleys with powerful torrents that have carved deep gorges and feed spectacular waterfalls.

luminous French Melanesia

154 top On both sides of Grande Terre, the principal island of New Caledonia, there are dozens of beaches of white sand rimmed by towering palms. The landscape is made all the more spectacular by the steep mountains rising on the horizon.

provoking a reaction from the Kanak tribes, who in 1878 engaged in a form of guerrilla warfare against the invaders. The French response was one of harsh repression, 150 villages being destroyed and their inhabitants being deported to the coasts and obliged to labor while their lands were ceded to new colonies. This cultural genocide obliterated the Kanak traditions as the 27,000 survivors of the original population of 70,000 were converted to Christianity. There was an inversion of this trend in the 1930s, and today the Kanak peoples live mainly in the north of the island and represent 42% of the archipelago's total population of 190,000 individuals, almost all of whom are concentrated on Grande Terre.

Whilst the capital Noumea—a modern city with large buildings, luxurious commercial centers and sophisticated French restaurants—is populated by a cosmopolitan mix of French (37% of the population), Polynesians from Wallis Island (another French possession near Samoa) and Tahiti (12%) and Asians (9%). In spite of the fact that the movement for self-rule has on a number of occasions obtained a majority of seats in the national assembly, New Caledonia remains French territory, the last European colony in Melanesia. The alternation of the Socialist carrot and the harshly wielded Gaullist stick has led to the struggle for independence being marred by massacres of natives and the unpunished assassinations of leaders. The archipelago has been militarized and Paris has no intention of letting it go, considering the production of nickel of strategic importance (in the manufacture of arms). The metal represents 90% of the archipelago's exports and its economic mainstay, although there is now a developing tourist industry.

154 center The Ile des Pins, situated around 43 miles to the south-east of Grande Terre, has a very complex coastline with large and small bays such as the one semi-enclosed by the Kuto peninsula, one of the pearls of the Pacific Ocean with incredible turquoise waters.

154 bottom The Ile des Pins is similar to Grande Terre in terms of the quality and variety of its flora as well as the geological composition of the terrain. The islands of New Caledonia are extremely fertile thanks to generous rainfall and volcanic soil.

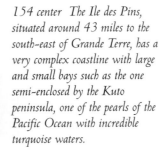

154-155 This enchanting beach is to be found on Ile des Pins which, together with Berlep, constitutes a geological extension of Grande Terre. The geology of these islands features superimposed strata of volcanic, sedimentary and morphological rocks.

155 bottom The Melanesian Kanak people, natives of the Ile des Pins, tackle the violent waves of the Pacific Ocean aboard traditional outrigger canoes fitted with sails. This type of navigation is widespread in much of Melanesia and Polynesia.

156 top Noumea, the capital of New Caledonia, is a modern and cosmopolitan city with large buildings, luxurious commercial centers and sophisticated French restaurants. The Italian architect, Renzo Piano, built the futuristic Jean-Marie Tjibao Cultural Center here in 1998.

156 center left The Kanak people of New Caledonia converted to Christianity following the defeat inflicted by the French in 1878 when the discovery of nickel encouraged the colonists to advance inland, provoking a reaction from the natives who engaged in a form of guerrilla warfare.

156 center right Christian missionaries arrived in New Caledonia in the first half of the nineteenth century, but only began to spread throughout the territory after it had been annexed in 1853. The first European to land in the archipelago was James Cook in 1774.

156 bottom The outrigger structure of the typical canoes of New Caledonia can clearly be seen in this photo. Prior to the colonization of the islands, these empirical but stable boats were the islanders sole means of transport and communication with the rest of the archipelago.

157 The islands of New Caledonia are rich in tropical plants. This photo depicts the coincidental flowering of the flamboyant and the bougainvillaea, this last botanical species being named in honor of the French explorer, Louis-Antoine Bougainville.

158-159 Ayers Rock is the world's largest monolith and is situated at the center of Australia. The rock is a sacred site for various Aboriginal tribes who live in the central regions of the continent and celebrate rites of initiation in its caverns and gorges.

158 bottom Two members of Australia's bizarre fauna have become symbols of the country: the kangaroo, the continent's most widespread animal and frequently identified as an emblem of the country itself, and the emu, the flightless bird representing the Australian version of the ostrich.

159 top A NASA satellite photo showing Australia, with the most easily recognizable part in red including the southern states of Victoria, South Australia and Western Australia. The northern regions are instead largely concealed by cloud formations.

159 bottom The stretch of coastline illustrated in this photo is to be found in the south of Australia where the process of erosion provoked by the violent ocean waves has carved the calcareous rocks into sometimes surreal landscapes.

In contrast with the myriad fragments of land that compose Polynesia, Micronesia and Melanesia, the western Pacific is dominated by the world's largest island, Australia. A continent with environments varying from the tropical to the temperate, in a territory—as large as the United States without Alaska—extending from the 10th parallel South, to the lower latitudes tormented by the Roaring Forties and populated by seals, sea lions and penguins. Australia was formed during the Jurassic Period of the Mesozoic Era as a consequence of the break-up of Gondwanaland, the Palaeozoic super-continent that incorporated South America, Antarctica, Africa, Madagascar, India, Arabia and Australia in a single land mass. The dismemberment of Gondwanaland was caused by the progressive shifting of the Afro-American tectonic plate towards the west, the Antarctic Plate towards the south and the Indo-Australian Plate to the east. Early in the Jurassic Period, around 200 million years ago, Australia was still part of a single land mass incorporating Southern Asia and Antarctica. The separation occurred just 150 million years ago. During the last Ice Age, which ended 10,000 years ago, isthmuses still linked the island to the Moluccas and New Guinea; it was by way of these natural land bridges that around 50,000 years ago the ancestors of the Aboriginals reached Australia. Despite being considered part of the New World, Australia is actually one of the planet's oldest areas of dry land. Much of it is composed of a thick layer of folded sedimentary rocks overlying a crystalline shield dating from the Precambrian time. The Flinders, Musgrave and MacDonnell ranges date back to a billion years. These mountains, eroded over time, are the only significant morphological variations to the vast plain that from the west to the center occupy three-quarters of the continent. Part of this immense plateau—with an average altitude of

AUSTRALIA: THE LARGEST ISLAND, THE SMALLEST CONTINENT

984 feet above sea level—is composed of depressions that around 120 million years ago were under water; below the Australian crust lie immense salt deposits as testified by the great salt lakes of southern Australia such as Lake Eyre. Situated 40 feet below sea level, this is the continent's largest depression; the fossilized remains of dinosaurs found in the salt show that in remote eras the region was covered with vegetation. The interior of the continent is known as the outback, a barren environment dominated by *spinifex*, thorny shrubs that are frequently bowled across the bare land by dust storms. The bush or outback is studded with a series of rock formations. Ayers Rock, the world's largest monolith, rises in the center of a flat plain. Katherine Canyon, actually a series of gorges, is located in the region of Alice Springs and was carved by rivers running between walls of red rock. The Pinnacles Desert in the south of Western Australia is punctuated by erect calcareous pillars while the Bungle Bungles of Kimberley in the north of Western Australia are a range of sandstone cones that form gorges filled with forests of palms.

Much of the interior is, however, covered with the dunes of white, red or golden sands of the Simpson, Great Victoria, Gibson and Great Sandy Deserts. The continent's eastern seaboard from the Cape York Peninsula to Tasmania, is instead bordered by the Great Dividing Range, a corrugated mountainous region separating the arid central and western lands from the fertile east coast where the most famous cities are situated and the great majority of the country's 18 million inhabitants are concentrated. The conformation of the territory, for the most part inhospitable desert plains, contributes to the great Australian paradox: this is the country with the lowest population density in the world—five inhabitants per square mile—but is also the most highly urbanized with four-fifths of the population living in the cities. In the south of New South Wales, Victoria and Tasmania, the mountain landscape is more vertical and majestic; the relief features in these areas are more recent and the last volcano was only extinguished 6,000 years ago. Here can be found the snow and the ski slopes of the Australian Alps (Victoria), the Snowy Mountains (New South Wales) and the Cradle Mountains (Tasmania), among which rises Mount Kosciusko, the highest peak on the continent at 7,314 feet. Along the Great Dividing Range, pockets of tropical jungle alternate with forests of eucalyptus, the tree that dominates the Australian landscape with over six hundred varieties, and areas of temperate rain forest such as that which covers broad areas of Tasmania, an island separated from the mainland during the last Ice Age. The temperate rain forest of Tasmania, one of the last three to survive world-wide, is very different to the humid jungle of the tropics. The taller trees are mostly pines such as the huon, an archaic tree with examples dating back 2,500 years. Pines represent the highest strata of the forest, whilst numerous varieties of ferns occupy the middle strata and mosses, fungi, moulds and lichens act as ground cover.

Australia has a massive, fairly regular form. The north-east coast features beaches fringed by coconut palms alternating with intricate mangrove forests. In the tract between the Tropic of Capricorn and Papua New Guinea, the east coast is flanked for 1,240 miles by the Great Barrier Reef, the worlds most varied marine ecosystem extending over an area just a little smaller than that of Great Britain and composed of hundreds of coral atolls and rocks. As well as over 1,400 varieties fish and 400 corals, the Australian reef is also home to thousands of species of sponges, sea urchins, molluscs and crustaceans, not to mention bizarre animals such as the dugong, six species of turtles and the deadly box jellyfish capable of killing a man in less than half a minute of direct contact.

160 top The Simpson Desert is located in South Australia on the border with the Northern Territory. This extremely arid terrain with sand dunes (the dark brown areas in this satellite photo) has average rainfall figures lower than those of the Sahara.

160 center The north coast of the Northern Territory and Melville and Bathurst Islands are subject to forest fires during the dry season. The darkest parts of this satellite photo taken indicate areas covered by mangroves.

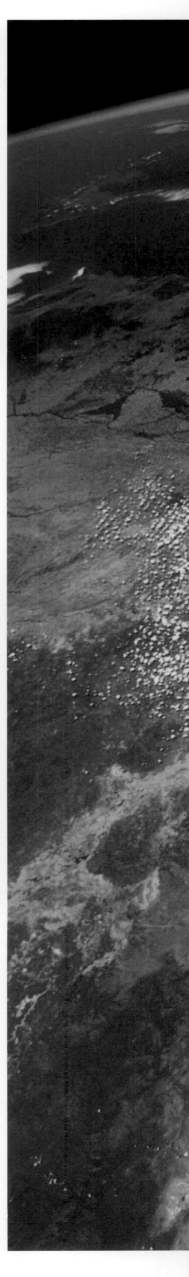

160 bottom This photo, taken by a NASA satellite, has captured a forest fire blazing in south-east Queensland, on the margins of a region close to Brisbane and adjacent to the Great Dividing Range, devoted to the cultivation of grain and the pasturing of cattle.

160-161 The south-east of Australia seen here in a NASA satellite photo with the whole of Victoria and around half of South Australia and New South Wales visible. Bottom right is Lake Eyre, Gulf St. Vincent where Adelaide is located, Kangaroo Island and the Yorke Peninsula.

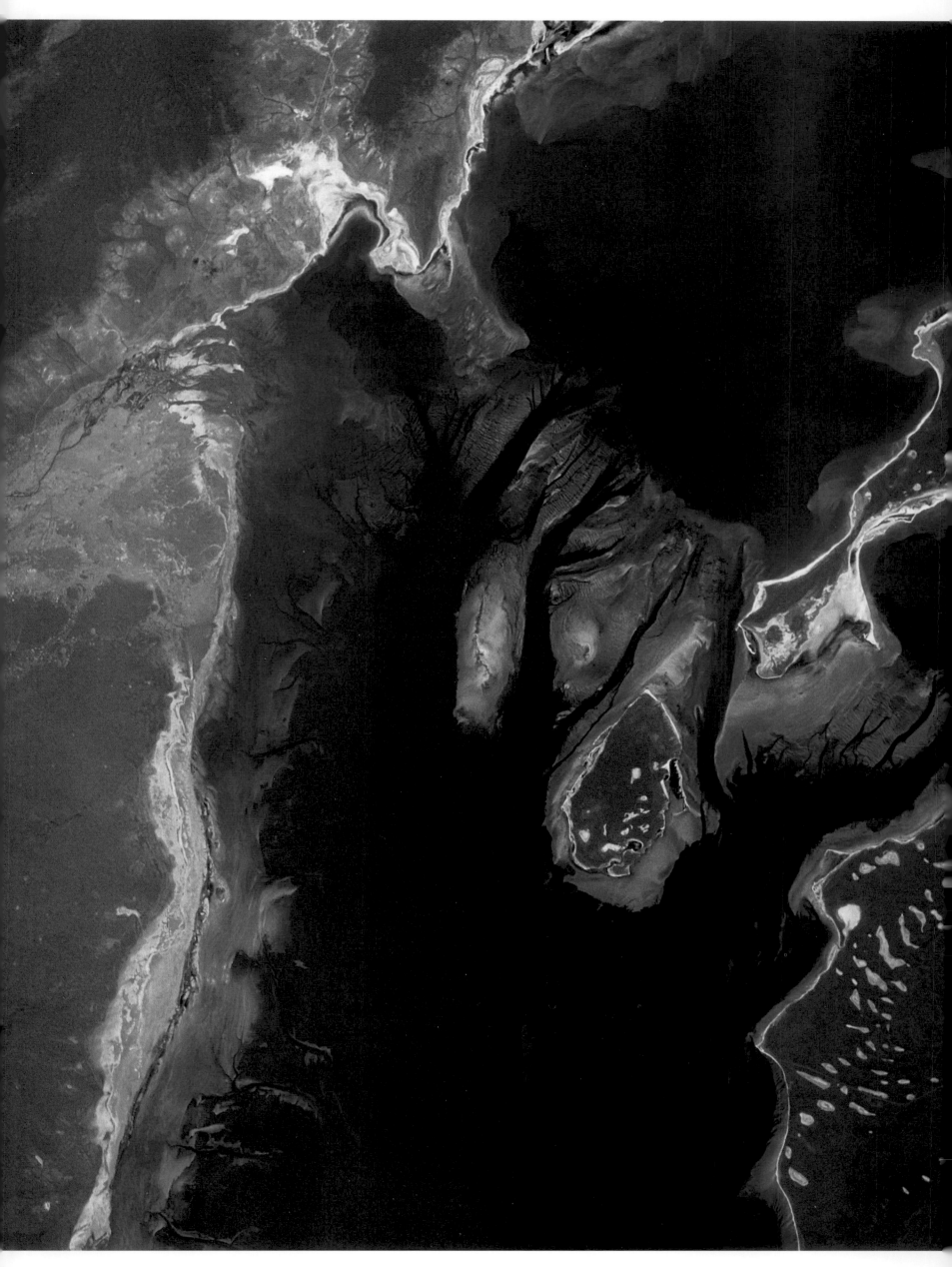

162 Shark Bay is located in the center of the coast of Western Australia. To the west of the estuary of the River Wooramel can be seen sand dunes and desert crests. The island highlighted in the photo is that of Faure in the center of Hamelin Pool.

163 top Another satellite photo, this showing Exmouth Gulf on the coast of Western Australia. The tongue of land on the right-hand side of the image is North West Cape. The area is surrounded by Ningaloo Reef, Australia's second largest barrier reef.

163 bottom This photo offers an oblique view of Shark Bay on the coast of Western Australia. Traces of a number of roads can be seen along the almost uninhabited shoreline, whilst Dirk Hartog Island and the Edel Peninsula can clearly be seen extending into the ocean.

The south-east coast, lacking the protection of the coral reef, is pounded by the ocean with powerful waves breaking on beaches locked between rocky outcrops creating innumerable bays. This is surfing territory, the Australian sport par excellence. Some hundreds of miles off the east coast, between New Zealand and New Caledonia, are two small islands that politically belong to Australia but which have much in common with the Polynesian landscapes and legends. Norfolk Island, located on the same latitude as Brisbane, is a rocky platform on which the heirs to the famous mutiny on the *Bounty* now live: they were transferred here in 1856 from Pitcairn Island in the Pacific between Tahiti and Easter Island. The magnificent Lord Howe Island is instead a fragment of land belonging to New South Wales but situated on the border between the cold Tasman Sea and the tropical Coral Sea. An island with green fields edged by cliffs falling sheer to the sea while on the other side gentle hills are grazed by herds of cows and the inhabitants play golf. At Lagoon Beach—enclosed by tropical vegetation and overlooked by a volcano—one might be in Polynesia with the lagoon and its coral reef populated by 100 species of coral and 500 different fish.

The continent's south coast is more irregular with the deep Spencer and Saint Vincent Gulfs, and the arc traced by the Great Australian Bight where schools of whales can frequently be spotted. The west coast proceeds northwards with infinite expanses of sand up to Ningaloo Reef, the country's second largest coral reef situated off Exmouth. From Broome to the Cape York Peninsula between the Timor and Arafura Seas, the north coast of Australia is the country's most rugged: deep bays and coasts suffocated by mangroves alternate with river mouths, marshes and immense swamps. This is the wildest region of the continent, one inhabited by hundreds of species of birds and the salt-water crocodile which may grow up to 23 feet long. Here, in the Top End of the Northern Territory, is the Kakadu National Park, the largest of the two thousand Australian parks that features the forests, marshes and waterfalls seen in the film

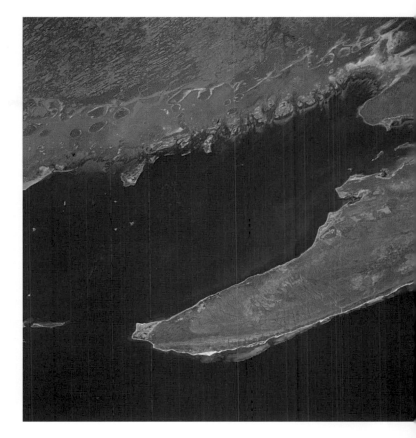

Crocodile Dundee.

Australia's isolation from the rest of the world has led to the evolution of remarkable flora and fauna. 85% of the plant species are endemic; that is to say, they only grow here. The animals are among the most archaic and bizarre in the world. Among the mammals the only placental species are the dingo—introduced 10,000 years ago from Indonesia—and a number of bats, whilst the scenario is dominated by dozens of species of marsupials, animals that, after a brief gestation period, complete their growth in a kind of open pouch on the mother's belly. The kangaroos, the common name with which forty-two species of *Macropodidae* are described, are joined by dozens of varieties of wallaby, smaller marsupials, some of which are so small that they can be mistaken for mice. This happened to the Dutchman Willem de Vlamingh who on landing in 1696 on an island off present-day Perth, called the place Rottnest or Rats' Nest, because it was inhabited by the quokka, micro-kangaroos with dark fur and the dimensions of a rat. The largest Australian family also includes around fifteen species of opossums, animals of varied shapes and sizes and resembling squirrels or small bears but all sharing nocturnal habits and an incurable curiosity. Yet another Australian marsupial is the koala, the small nocturnal bear-like animal that spends all its life perched among the branches of the eucalyptus trees, on the leaves of which it depends for food and liquid. The wombat is a less elegant animal, fat and clumsy, the size of a small pig. The continent is home to four species of wombats which live in the temperate forests of the south-eastern regions and dig their burrows among the roots of the trees. The very few surviving carnivorous marsupials include the quoll (similar to a squirrel) and the Tasmanian Devil (a predator the size of a small dog). The members of the Monotremata order are even more primitive than that of the marsupials. These animals lay eggs, defecate and urinate from a single orifice, hatch their eggs like reptiles and nurse their young by soaking the hairs on their abdomens with milk because they have mammary glands but not nipples. The order includes the duck-billed platypus with falcon-like claws and the echidna, a hedgehog with a cigar-shaped snout.

164 top A NASA satellite photo illustrating the concentration of phytoplankton in the north-western waters of the Coral Sea. The most intensive production of micro-organisms in the Pacific Ocean has been recorded around the Great Barrier Reef.

164 bottom left Swain Reef is one of the southernmost formations of the Great Barrier Reef that, composed of around 2,600 banks of coral, extends for about 1,240 miles from the north-east of Australia to Papua New Guinea.

164 bottom right The northern coast of Queensland features in this satellite photo, with the forested mountains of the Great Dividing Range separating the fertile, cultivated coastal regions from the semi-arid plains of the interior.

164-165 King Sound is situated on the north-west coast of Australia. In this satellite photo the sedimentation transported to the sea from the Kimberley Plateau by the Fitzroy river can be seen. Roebuck Bay (top right) houses the city of Broome.

166 top *Obiri Rock, situated in the Kakadu National Park (Northern Territory), features some of the most notable Aboriginal graffiti and rock paintings. Forms of artistic expression that depict men and animals and which according to Carbon 14 dating were completed 23,000 years ago.*

166-167 *Many Aboriginal tribes from the north of Australia still live in the traditional manner, practicing the rituals of the Dream Time, their creation myth based on a totemic geography that identifies ancestors in the various elements of the landscape.*

167 top Many Aboriginals live in the city suburbs, above all in Sydney. They rarely integrate with the western lifestyle and more frequently survive in ramshackle homes thanks to state unemployment subsidies while trying to cope with the twin scourges of a poor diet and rampant alcoholism.

167 bottom This Aboriginal graffiti was discovered on rock at Kimberley, Western Australia. The most recent analyses using Carbon 14 testing have demonstrated that the continent's earliest rock paintings date back 53,000 years and are the oldest found anywhere in the world.

Aboriginals: the dream time nomads

A stripe as black as their skins, another as red as the earth to which they are bound and, in the middle, a circle as yellow as the sun that gives them life. The Aboriginal flag, the symbol of the pride and resurrection of one of the most mistreated peoples in history. In 1788, early in the colonization of the country, Australia was declared *terra nullius*, or uninhabited. As far as the British colonists were concerned, the naked, black-skinned beings with snub noses and prominent torsos who chased kangaroos through the bush were beasts, not men. According to the official accounts, when, in 1788, Captain Arthur Phillip landed at Port Jackson—the present-day Sydney—with a thousand soldiers and convicts to found the British crown's new penal colony, around 300,000 Aboriginals were living in Australia. This is contested by various sources; research conducted at the University of Melbourne, for example, claims that the Aboriginals numbered one and a half million, one of the numerous historical revisions that have taken place over the last twenty years in a country pervaded by guilt and thirsty for history.

The Aboriginals have lived in Australia for around 50,000 years. During the last Ice Age, black peoples of Dravidian origin reached the island-continent from India by way of the tongue of dry land that still united Australia, New Guinea and the Moluccas. What is certain is that the Vedda tribe, the oldest ethnic group in Asia, semi-nomadic Negro cavern dwellers, settled on the islands and the Gulf of Carpentaria on the north coast of the continent. The Lardils of Mornington Island are probably their direct descendants. From the northern coast, the Aboriginals spread throughout the continent and sub-divided into 500 tribes. Their hunter-gatherer economy obliged them to undertake perpetual migrations in order to find wells, follow the movements of animals and to reach areas seasonally rich in fruits. Within each clan composed of thirty or forty individuals, there was a division of labor based on sex and age. The men hunted kangaroos, wallabies, emus (the Australian relative of the ostrich), porcupines and ant-eaters with pointed spears that in central Australia were launched via a throwing stick. The boomerang which has become a symbol of the Aboriginals in the collective imagination, was invented 10,000 years ago and was used by certain tribes in the central deserts to hunt birds and small marsupials. During hunting trips a rich gestural alphabet allowed the hunters to signal the type of prey spotted to their companions without alarming the game. The women and children were responsible for the gathering of fruits and berries and also of worms and larvae, thus guaranteeing the daily supply of food that hunting, inevitably governed by the

movements of the herds, was unable to provide. The limitations of hunting were aggravated by the Aboriginals' inability to store and preserve food. Due to their nomadic habits, the Aboriginals did not build huts but rather fashioned temporary shelters with branches and the skins of marsupials. Nomadism permeated every aspect of Aboriginal culture, beginning with the Dream Time, the Aboriginal creation myth. Dream Time is a legendary era in which the Ancestors—giant beings in the form of kangaroos, emus or serpents—modelled the landscape with their songs and gave life to the plants, the animals and to man. They subsequently returned to earth and assumed the appearance of rocks, trees or other elements in the environment. This is why many tribes in central Australia regard the components of the landscape as elements of a totemic geography. Mountains, caves, wells, rivers, dunes and stars are all creation scenes and aspects of the Ancestors: ancestral paths that the Aboriginals must cover in order to perpetuate the Dream Time. The majority of the tribes lived isolated from the rest of the world for tens of

thousands of years and the sparse presence of Man in the immense Australian territory led to the development of 270 languages, all deriving from the Austroneasian stock. The various tribes maintained relationships with each other by way of the *corroboree*, occasions for the exchange of songs and dances, for the bartering of objects as useless as they were symbolic and for the concession of rights of transit along their respective creation paths, along the lines of natural wells that guaranteed survival in the desert. A fundamental element of inter-tribal communications was for thousands of years the walkabout, a nomadic practice that still today leads the men of diverse tribes to abandon their families and follow—sometimes for long periods—an ancestral path, frequently with the sole aim of meeting a single perhaps unknown person. A wanderlust that is as inexplicable as it is irresistible and that is today seen as an obstacle to the employment of Aboriginals: once gripped by the nomadic drive they will leave their jobs with no advance warning, throwing the European entrepreneurs into disarray. The Aboriginals' only relationship with the outside world was that of certain northern tribes with Macassan fishermen and traders from the island of Sulawesi in Indonesia. Communications between the diverse tribes and with other peoples was the evolutionary key for a population rooted in the Palaeolithic age. Through contacts with Asian peoples, the tribes of the torrid northern seaboard developed arts, knowledge and elaborate rituals. The Tiwis of Melville Island (to the North of Darwin) had a complex social system based on polygamy and funerary ceremonies. These customs featured extreme respect for the elders of the tribe who spent their last years in the company of young girls and who were buried with dances and extremely tall and brightly painted ritual altars. The Tiwis, like the Lardils, fished and sailed crude rafts. The tribes of Arnhem Land developed concepts similar to the Ying and Yang of Eastern philosophy, handed down knowledge orally during special ceremonies, used decorated hollow tree trunks as ossuaries and depicted reality and dreams in paintings on bark. The majority of graffiti and rock paintings are to be found in the North of the country: from the incisions of Obiri Rock at Kakadu to those of the Quinkan caves on Cape York. Scrapers of quartzite and hematite pigment found in Arnhem Land have been attributed an age of 53,000 years, thanks to Carbon 14 dating, and are the oldest "artistic" tools ever discovered anywhere in the world. Graffiti and bark paintings are much more advanced works than the ephemeral drawings in sand made by the nomads of the central deserts. They depicted routes between wells, the creation myth and everyday reality. The life-style of the Aboriginals of the deserts was particularly gruelling and

168 top The Northern Territory is the Australian state with the highest percentage of Aboriginal inhabitants (almost a quarter of the total population) and some of the liveliest folklore events, such as the Yendumu and Barunga festivals and the works of the desert artists.

168-169 The Olgas rock formation is situated at the center of the continent, close to the more famous Ayers Rock. The Olgas group is composed of 36 monoliths, with rounded surfaces that form a kind of labyrinth criss-crossed by a network of footpaths.

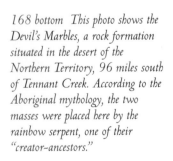

168 bottom This photo shows the Devil's Marbles, a rock formation situated in the desert of the Northern Territory, 96 miles south of Tennant Creek. According to the Aboriginal mythology, the two masses were placed here by the rainbow serpent, one of their "creator-ancestors."

169 bottom King's Canyon is the largest gorge in central Australia, excavated by the erosive forces of the rivers flowing in the George Gill Range. The most spectacular area is known as the Lost City (in the photo) with its red domes of calcareous origins.

170 *The koala has arboreal habits. The attractive marsupial bear spends its days perched among the branches and feeding on the leaves of 35 species of eucalyptus, from which it obtains all its nourishment and the liquids necessary for its survival.*

171 top *The frilled lizard (Chlamydosaurus kingii) is one of the most bizarre reptiles of the Australian desert with its scaly ruff around its neck. This animal is on average 18 inches long and has an extraordinary ability to camouflage itself.*

comparable only with that of the bushmen of the Kalahari Desert in southern Africa. Even more primitive were the tribes of Tasmania, as the separation of the island from the continent (around 12,000 years ago) deprived them of any cultural contacts. They lived naked in a harsh climate and because they were unable to reproduce fire they were obliged to carry a glowing coal with them at all times. They had neither boomerangs nor throwing sticks and used stones and extremely long spears for hunting. The Tasmanian tribes were the closest of the Australian Aboriginals to the Stone Age and were the first to suffer from the white invasion: seventy years after the arrival of the first colonists they were extinct. A similar fate awaited the majority of the tribes of the fertile coastal regions of southern Australia as they were decimated by the diseases imported by the British and their bloody territorial expansionism. The Aboriginals' right to life was not recognized until the passing of the Aboriginal Act in 1860, by which time only 50,000 individuals survived, scattered across the central deserts and in the forests of the north. In the south the few survivors were dressed and taken to the missions to be civilized. A few decades later this was the

destiny of all the native Australians, as with the Assimilation Laws the deserts were combed and all the Aboriginals were enclosed in order to be given a Western education. The children born of the relationships between black women and white men were taken away from the mothers; the traumas deriving from these laws are the fabric of the autobiographical novel *My Place* by Sally Morgan, a best-seller in Australia in the late Eighties. This book has been one of the pillars of the Aboriginal revival which began to gather strength from the 1970s onwards, thanks to the Land Rights movement which demanded the return of the tribes' ancestral lands. The policy of assimilation was abandoned in 1967 with a referendum that granted the Aboriginals the right to citizenship. Having lost their cultural roots, many Aboriginals moved to peripheral urban areas where they lived on state unemployment subsidies and alcoholism was rife. The Aboriginals—today they number 265,000 and represent 1.5% of the Australian population— remain the country's poorest social class, have a lower life expectancy than the whites and suffer from diabetes and cardiac diseases due to their changed diet and the abuse of alcohol. In 1976, a program of land restitution was set underway and has so far returned around an eighth of the total national territory to the tribes. In 1994, the Mabo sentence— which takes its name from a stubborn Aboriginal from Murray Island—passed by the High Court of Brisbane denied the principal of *terra nullius* and confirmed the Aboriginals' rights over their native land. This sentence has been challenged by breeders and the mineral extraction industries who fear the expropriation of their property, arguments that fed the recent success of the racist One Nation party founded by Pauline Hanson. Alongside the political legitimization there has been a development of Aboriginal culture expressed through literature, film, theater and above all figurative art. The acrylic paintings of the artists of the central deserts have conquered the art market and even been shown in the famous Webber Gallery in New York, creating a bridge whereby the Aboriginals are finally able to communicate with the rest of the world.

171 center left *Kangaroos are the most well known members of the marsupial order, that is to say animals that after a brief period of gestation, complete their development in a kind of open pouch on their mother's belly. Almost all the Australian mammals belong to this archaic order.*

171 center right *This photo shows the head of an emu (Dromaius novaehollandiae), the Australian relative of the ostrich. The emu is a flightless bird that lives in the forests and the grassy plains where it feeds on shoots, leaves, flowers, fruits, berries and all kinds of insects.*

171 bottom *This photo shows an emu in the bush as the Australian interior is known. In spite of the fact that it is flightless, this bird is capable of moving very quickly, reaching up to 31 mph when running, and is an excellent swimmer. The emu completes annual migrations in search of food.*

172 top The atoll of Heron Island is a natural park visited by birdwatching enthusiasts because the forest is home to 50,000 examples of dozens of feathered species. During the migration season between October and March the bird population rises to 200,000.

172-173 Heron Island, the southernmost island of the Great Barrier Reef, is a minuscule atoll covered with rain-forest vegetation and embraced by a ring of white sand.

173 top The Great Barrier Reef, situated off the northern coast of Queensland, is the largest and most complex marine ecosystem on the planet. It is home to 400 species of coral and thousands of species of fish, crustaceans and invertebrates.

173 bottom The Great Barrier Reef has an enormous backwash. 98 percent of its banks of coral occupy a surface area similar to that of Great Britain and since 1975 have been part of a protected reserve after having been declared a national marine park.

174-175 Hook Island, in the Whitsunday group, is almost completely covered with tropical vegetation surrounding white sand beaches.

Queensland:

more lazily aboard glass-bottomed boats or miniature submarines that dive amidst the corals. Visitors are faced with a breathtaking scene: below the surface brilliantly colored fish swim around madreporic structures of the most bizarre forms. It is even more spectacular seen from the sky, the waves breaking and foaming on the seemingly endless reef. A wall of coral encloses a turquoise lagoon lined with sandy beaches consolidated by coconut palms. The marvels of the landscape go hand-in-hand with the hospitality of the islands scattered along the 1,240-mile length of the reef. Natural paradises such as Heron Island, a Lilliputian island enclosed by a band of talcum white on which green turtles lay their eggs. Exclusive resorts such as Lizard Island are frequented by the likes of Prince Charles, Tom Cruise and Nicole Kidman. Ports of call for sailing enthusiasts such as

beaches, corals and cowboys

With palm-fringed beaches, myriad tropical islands and the stunning underwater spectacle of the Great Barrier Reef, Queensland offers the most attractive marine image of a country that has made its beaches its calling card. It is, however, the Australian state with the highest growth rate, the giant that with its enormous mineral, agricultural and touristic resources, supports the Australian economy even during periods of recession. Cairns in northern Queensland is the Antipodean city that has grown fastest over the last decade, thanks to the boom in tourists visiting the Great Barrier Reef and its islands. Thousands of young people stop here, seduced by the rock rhythms put out by the pubs and discotheques, while just as many wealthy tourists spend their days browsing its shopping centers. To the north of Cairns, past Port Douglas—the most beautiful beach of the entire coastline and frequented by the Formula 1 drivers prior to the Melbourne Grand Prix—one reaches the Daintree River which is inhabited by salt-water crocodiles. The locals recount stories and/or myths about the visitors torn to pieces by the beasts on the banks of the river. The *crocs*, as they are called here, can reach up to 23 feet in length and will attack buffalo and kangaroos and, given the opportunity, man. To the north of the river, around Cape Tribulation, the rain forest dominates with its mosses, lichens, lianas, ferns and imposing strangling figs. From here, following the coast, one reaches Cooktown, a city founded in 1873 by the pioneers who found gold in the Palmer River. Once the seam of gold had been exhausted the city began to decline. Its population fell from a peak of 50,000 to little more than a thousand and it was tormented by hurricanes and sank into the damp torpor that cloaks the region. Cooktown is the last major settlement before the jigsaw puzzle of jungle, desolate plains and swamps of the Cape York Peninsula, linked to the rest of the country by a track that is virtually unpassable during the rainy season. The rest of the year it is used by the few trucks supplying the Aboriginal communities such as Laura, a small village that each year stages the Cape York Aboriginal Dance Festival, an opportunity for the various tribes of the region to meet. The festival features authentic native culture, as does Kuranda, the town in the hills above Cairns that since 1987 has been the home of the Tjapukai Dance Theatre, the most famous Aboriginal theater company. The 70 islands that between Cape York and Papua New Guinea form the Torres Strait archipelago are instead inhabited by people of Melanesian origin.

Cairns is the main base for visiting the Great Barrier Reef in order to explore the coral world with masks and flippers, or

the Whitsundays, an archipelago of 74 hilly islands cloaked in vegetation and featuring an infinite series of promontories, beaches and bays. And economic destinations for backpackers such as Magnetic Island. To the south of the Barrier Reef lies Fraser Island, the world's largest sand island, inhabited by dingoes and where hundreds of milk white dunes enclose turquoise lakes. There is also, however, the Queensland of the outback ranchers, the remote interior. It can be experienced at Rockhampton, the terminus for the livestock convoys. From here the tracks follow the Tropic of Capricorn as far as Longreach, crossing immense farms inhabited by men who still drive their herds on horseback. In reality, the livestock is today rounded up firstly with small aircraft that fly so low over the cattle they almost graze their backs. Land Rovers and trial bikes are then used to herd the animals into the corrals. From the farms the cattle are ferried to the railway stations in road-trains, three-trailer trucks capable of carrying up to 200 animals that can be spotted on the plains dozens of miles away. From the outback to Brisbane, the capital and modern facet of Queensland, the interface between the wild interior and the futuristic metropolises of the south, skyscrapers, highways and pedestrian zones in which kids in school uniforms blend into the cosmopolitan crowds. The city is located on the Gold Coast, the series of sandy beaches linking Brisbane to the border with New South Wales. Surfers Paradise, the coast's most important center, is the favorite destination of honeymooning Japanese couples as well as the dream of Tokyo office workers who—attracted by the prices, climate and golf courses—buy apartments here for their retirement. Here the myth of deserted beaches and boundless spaces of Australia gives way to the glass and concrete reality of the skyscrapers that trace the horizon.

176-177 The magnificent
Whitehaven beach on Whitsunday
Island is the largest in the
archipelago of the same name. The
island group is Queensland's most
numerous, with 74 hilly rock
islands for the most part cloaked in
luxuriant tropical vegetation.

176 bottom The Whitsunday
archipelago represents Australian
sailing enthusiasts' destination of
choice. Its intriguing scenery is
composed of a series of islands (the
majority uninhabited), bays, inlets,
promontories, stacks and channels.

177 top An aerial photo offering
an even more spectacular view of
Whitehaven beach. In the
Whitsunday archipelago,
uninhabited, environmentally
unspoilt islands Such as Hook and
Long Islands alternate with others
boasting luxurious resorts such as
Hayman and Lindeman Islands.

177 bottom The chromatic and
environmental contrasts between the
turquoise lagoon protected by the
Great Barrier Reef, and the deep
blue of the ocean flecked with the
white foam of waves breaking on the
coral, are highlighted in this aerial
photo.

178 top The Atherton Tableland is a 93-mile-long plateau situated in the mountains to the west of Cairns in the north of Queensland. Peopled in the late nineteenth century by Scottish immigrants, it is to a large extent covered by artificial pine forests which alternate with tropical vegetation.

178 center The galah (Cacatua roseicapilla) is one of the most common birds of Australia where almost 800 species of birds have been recorded. The galah belongs to the Cacatuidae family and is a form of parrot present on the continent in around a dozen different species.

178 bottom Hamilton Island is the most tourist-oriented of the Whitsunday group, having been transformed in the 1970s into a holiday center with numerous hotels, commercial areas, an airport and a heliport. The island nonetheless retains spectacular beaches of white sand.

178-179 Mossman Gorge is a canyon in the north of Queensland in which large parts are occupied by dense rain-forest, the remains of the immense damp jungles that 100 million years ago covered the southern regions of the supercontinent Gondwanaland.

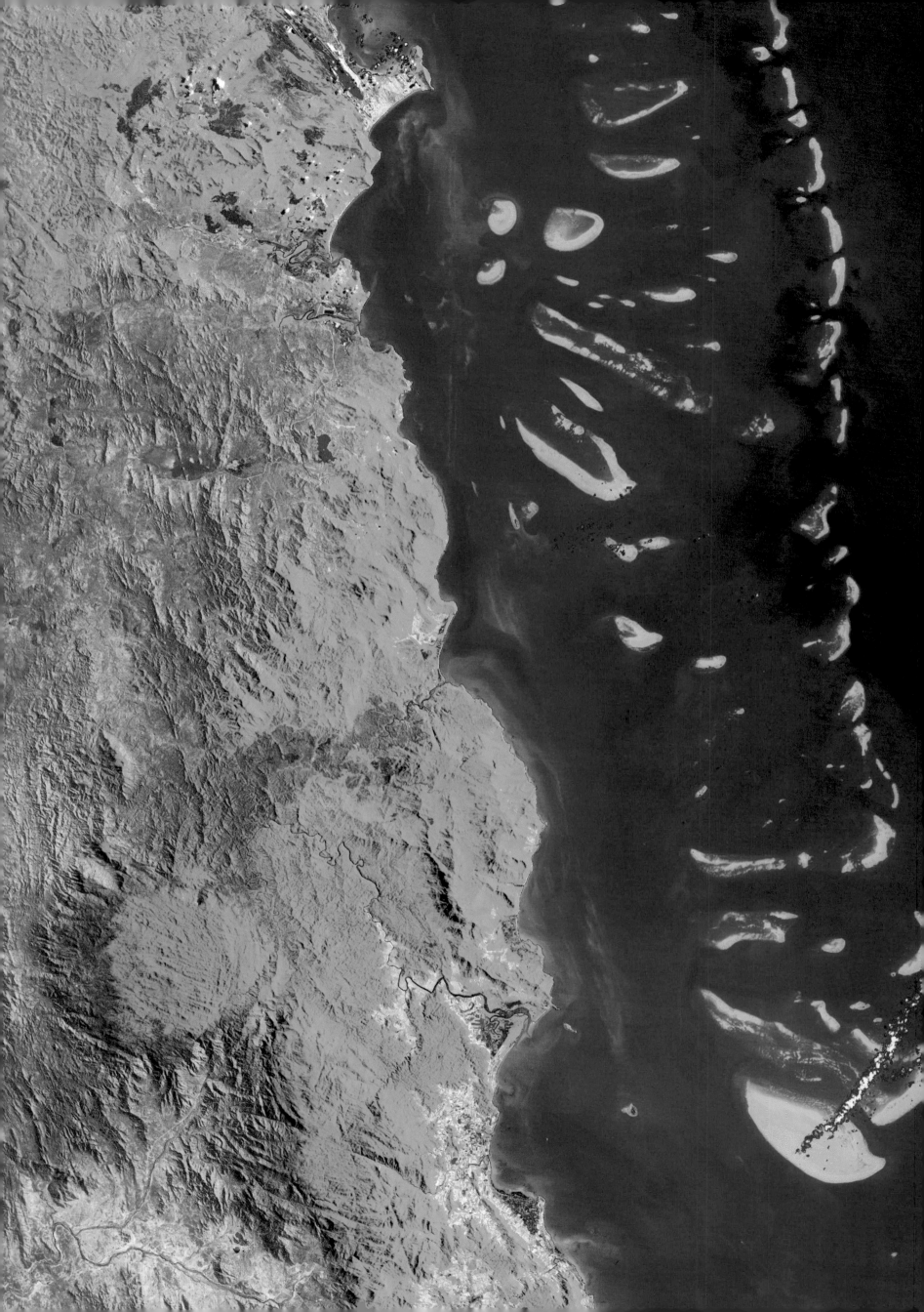

180 *A NASA satellite photo showing the geological singularity of northern Queensland. The pink areas are the relief features of the Great Dividing Range and the green the coastal plains. The patches that can be seen in the ocean are instead the coral banks of the Great Barrier Reef.*

181 *At the bottom of the photo can be seen the Story Bridge of Brisbane which links the commercial and financial center of the city to Kangaroo Point. Beyond the skyscrapers can be seen the extensive exhibition and recreational area of the South Bank.*

The modern history of Australia began on the coasts of New South Wales. In 1770, James Cook landed in a bay to the south of present-day Sydney: he officially discovered Australia and claimed possession of the territory on behalf of the British crown. He named the inlet Botany Bay after he had catalogued hundreds of unknown plant and animal species in just a few days. A few years later, in 1788, Arthur Phillip landed at Port Jackson—now Sydney—with a thousand convicts, thus creating New South Wales, the United Kingdom's new penal colony. The first settlement rose around the bay where the Opera House now stands. Where the ships moored at the Rocks, the tents soon gave way to wooden shacks, hovels frequented by prostitutes, criminals and rum smugglers. Two centuries later, the landscape has been completely transformed, with the skyscrapers of the City encircling Port Jackson and the middle class suburbs on the north shore, but Sydney remains the country's principal gateway. The continent's most attractive city is eccentric and cosmopolitan with a population composed of 140 different ethnic groups enjoying an enviable lifestyle that is more open, lively and carefree than in any other part of Australia. Beaches, sailing, markets, boutiques, art galleries and exciting night-life are all part of the Sydney scene which rather than reflecting the harsher and wilder aspects of the Antipodes prefers the Australian good life fable. Sydney is one of the planet's most modern metropolises with the monorail running between the skyscrapers of the center,

182 This beach can be found at Byron Bay, a town situated in the north of New South Wales, on a promontory separating long sand banks beaten by the violent waves of the Pacific Ocean. It represents the easternmost tip of the Australian continent.

183 top This photo shows the green southern coastline of Sydney. The large inlet to the south of the city was baptized Botany Bay due to the extraordinary variety of the local flora. To the south of the bay can be found the Royal National Park, Australia's first protected nature reserve.

183 center Bondi Beach is the most famous stretch of coastline in Sydney, frequented by surfing enthusiasts who ride the violent Pacific rollers balanced on frail boards. Teams of muscular lifeguards stationed on the beach are ready to save those in difficulty in the water.

New South Wales: the cradle of Australia

183 bottom left The ocean coast of Sydney can be seen in this photo. The city has a population of almost 4 million and between Port Jackson and Botany Bay has a coastline of almost 25 miles with rocky cliffs alternating with beaches and areas equipped as public parks.

183 bottom right Numerous seal communities live on the south coast of New South Wales. Australia has two species of this marine mammal, the Australian Artocephalus doriferus and the New Zealand Artocephalus forsteri restricted to Kangaroo Island.

the road tunnel crossing the bay and a high-tech panoramic tower standing 1000 feet tall; with Darling Harbor, the old port transformed into a multi-functional center with commercial, sports, museum and exhibition facilities; with the environmentally friendly Olympic village constructed on the banks of the Parramatta River for the 2000 Olympic Games that after the event will become a residential suburb; and with the Opera House, the masterpiece of Jorn Utzon, that overlooks the bay in a succession of billowing sails evoking the sailing ships of the first European explorers of the Pacific.

There is, however, more to New South Wales than just Sydney, in spite of the fact that the city accounts for over half of its 6,200,000 inhabitants (over a third of the entire Australian population). Morphologically the state is divided into three regions: the densely populated coastal zones, the mountains of the Great Dividing Range and the desolate interior that, to the west of the ridge, occupies two thirds of the state's territory.

The immense desert plain was seen for the first time in 1813 by the pioneers who crossed the Blue Mountains; today these beautiful mountains can be reached in an hour by train from Sydney and are one of the city dwellers' favourite weekend retreats. The outback is instead characterized by the rugged face of Broken Hill, the mining town founded in 1883 on the border with South Australia following the discovery of the world's greatest silver and zinc deposits. The seams were exhausted by 1985 and today Broken Hill is just one of the anonymous ranchers' towns in a state that, despite the futuristic appearance of Sydney, is home to two-fifths of all the sheep in Australia, around 60 million animals or ten per head of human population. The contrasts continue with grey industrial towns such as Newcastle and, in a state of rough sheep breeders, ruthless traders

and rampant managers, the largest hippie community in the Antipodes. Close to the border with Queensland lies the Rainbow Area, a region of beaches, green hills and virgin forests surrounding Byron Bay. Dominated by a lighthouse, this is the easternmost tip of the continent. Following the Aquarius Festival of Nimbin (a small inland village in the area) here in 1973, a kind of Australian Woodstock, the region witnessed a "return to the land" of Sydney and Melbourne's alternative community. There would be nothing unusual in this were it not for the fact that crossing the region today involves flashbacks to the Seventies and the rock concerts, the marijuana and the dreams and utopias of that generation. To the south of Byron Bay, along a coastline characterized by long sandy beaches and a subtropical climate, are the seaside towns of Coffs Harbor and Port Macquarie. The former, founded as a center of the timber industry, features the Great Banana, a 33-foot-long fibreglass sculpture, one of the many "Big Things," gigantic installations scattered throughout the country celebrating *Aussie* animals and products.

From the jungles and beaches of the north to the ski slopes of the Snowy Mountains, New South Wales represents a distinct frontier between tropical and temperate Australia. In the cooler regions of the south of the state can be found the Australian Capital Territory and Canberra, the capital built from scratch halfway between Sydney and Melbourne in order to put an end to their rivalry. After independence in 1901, it took forty years for Walter Burley Griffin's project for a green, liveable city to come to fruition. Canberra revolves around an artificial lake set in parks; it is dominated by a 460-foot-high water spout and divides the city into two sectors.

To the north is the commercial zone, to the south the new parliament, surrounded by a network of freeways linking the public buildings to the residential quarters benefiting from a urban plan that demanded 8 million trees in a city of 300,000 inhabitants.

184-185 Lord Howe Island is extraordinarily beautiful. It belongs to New South Wales despite being located 435 miles east of the Australian coast. Due to its unique environment, in 1982 it was added to UNESCO's World Heritage List.

184 bottom The rocks of Neds Beach on Lord Howe Island are coated with brilliant green algae. Thanks to a microclimate with temperatures of between 75 and 104° F and frequent rain, the island boasts a great variety of endemic plants including the kentia palm.

185 top The basalt walls of Mount Lidgbird (an extinct volcano) contrast with the green pastures and are reflected in a blue lagoon enclosed by a barrier reef composed of 94 species of coral. 490 species of fish have been recorded in the lagoon.

185 bottom Situated on the confine between the Tasman and the Coral Seas, Lord Howe Island has an oceanic side covered with green pastures and a lagoon side featuring sub-tropical vegetation and rimmed by long beaches of white sand.

186 top Sydney's central business district is composed of glass and concrete skyscrapers of the most bizarre forms. The 1000-foot-high Sydney Tower rises above all the other buildings and boasts two restaurants on revolving platforms that offer spectacular views over the entire city.

186 center George Street is the main city artery in the center of Sydney. It starts from the Rocks, cuts through the central business district and crosses Haymarket and the Chinatown area before joining Broadway, where the student quarter of Glebe and the working class district of Redfern begin.

186-187 The Opera House is the symbol of Sydney. It was designed by the Dane, Jorn Utzon, and completed by a group of Australian architects. It was under construction for 14 years. The multi-purpose center houses four theaters as well as shops and restaurants.

187 bottom left Sydney developed around Port Jackson. To the north of the bay are middle class residential suburbs linked to the city center on the south side by Sydney Harbor Bridge and a road tunnel.

187 bottom right The city of Sydney is full of architectural contrasts. Nineteenth century churches and buildings are reflected in the glass walls of futuristic skyscrapers. The old Queen Victoria Building has instead been transformed into a modern shopping center.

186 bottom The beach and the resort community of Manly are located on the north side of Port Jackson close to North Head (which once housed quarantined immigrants), the peninsula which with South Head forms the strait whereby Port Jackson and Sydney are linked to the Pacific Ocean.

Victoria: skyscrapers,

188 top left Melbourne Town Hall is situated at the corner of Collins and Swanston Streets in the heart of the city, an area composed of an ordered grid-pattern of streets. The central business district which developed at the time of the gold rush has been nicknamed the Golden Mile.

188 top right This photo shows the city of Melbourne seen from the Yarra River which cuts through the city. On the east bank lie the

Botanic Gardens (to the south) and the sports facilities (to the north), constructed on the occasion of the 1956 Olympic Games.

188-189 Ninety Mile Beach is the immensely long stretch of sand that runs along the coast of the Hopetoun Channel to Lakes Entrance in Gippsland, the coastal region of the state of Victoria that extends to the east of Melbourne as far as the border with New South Wales.

penguins and smart races

Founded by free colonists rather than deported convicts, Victoria is the most European of the Australian states. So close were its ties to the motherland that it named its capital after the current Prime Minister of Great Britain, Lord Melbourne. Following the Second World War it became the preferred destination of immigrants from the Mediterranean countries. In spite of its relatively small size—it is the smallest of the continental states—its greater population density (around 51 inhabitants per square mile) and its undisputed industrial vocation, it is home to the most important national myths and an infinite series of natural attractions: the small Philip Island on whose beaches hundreds of penguins land each evening, the forests rich in fauna of the Wilson Promontory, the green hills of the south dotted with millions of grazing sheep, the Great Ocean Road, the highway linking Melbourne to South Australia along the continent's most spectacular coastline. In Port Campbell National Park the scenery is enriched by the so-called Twelve Apostles, towering stacks rising from the ocean breaker, and a rocky promontory, London Bridge, featuring two enormous arches leading out into the sea. Further inland, the landscape is dominated by the south-west foothills of the Great Dividing Range, the Grampians, covered with forests of eucalyptus, conifers and ferns from which sandstone peaks emerge. This natural reserve features a dense network of footpaths and is inhabited by koalas, kangaroos, wallabies and opossums. In the eastern regions of the state, the Great Dividing Range is instead represented by the Victoria Alps with peaks up to 6,560 feet high equipped with alpine skiing runs. These valleys were once the haunt of Ned Kelly, a bandit transformed into a national hero. In 1877, in the forests of the Wombat Mountains (named after a marsupial the size of a small pig which inhabits the area), Kelly formed a gang of brigands known as the Bushrangers, becoming a symbol of the resurrection of the poor farmers among whom he grew up; a kind of Robin Hood who robbed the rich while evading the forces of law and order. Hundreds of police officers were sent after Kelly, but it was three years before they eventually caught up with him, thanks to the help of an informer. He was hanged in Melbourne on the 11th of November, 1880. Together with Eureka Stockade and Phar Lap (an invincible thoroughbred), Ned Kelly is a key figure in Australian folklore. The Eureka Stockade episode at Ballarat was the only time the Australians rebelled against the authority of the British crown. Following the discovery of gold in Victoria, the miners protested at the imposition of a mining tax, a small band coming into conflict with the British troops. Eventually the tax was abolished. The

189 top The Houses of Parliament of the State of Victoria (located in Spring Street) constitute, together with the nearby monumental buildings of the Windsor Hotel and the Princess Theater, Melbourne's most important examples of Victorian architecture.

189 center For decades the port of Melbourne was the gateway to Australia for millions of European immigrants. The capital of Victoria is a multi-ethnic city with numerous Greek, Italian and Lebanese communities, above all in the Carlton and Fitzroy quarters.

189 bottom St. Patrick's Cathedral is situated behind the Fitzroy Gardens, the site of Captain Cook Cottage, the home of the discoverer of Australia, transported and rebuilt here after having been dismantled brick by brick in England.

190-191 The Twelve Apostles represents one of the most spectacular stretches of the Great Ocean Road, a coastal artery to the west of Melbourne offering breathtaking scenery and rock formations such as the London Bridge, a double arch plunging into the sea.

third Australian legend is even more bizarre: Phar Lap, a horse that began racing in 1929 and in the course of three years proceeded to win more races than any other horse in the history of the sport. The story illustrates the passion for racing of Victoria's population: the state boasts over 400 betting shops and the Melbourne Cup is the most important race, as well as Australia's premier social event. Apart from the race itself and the 130 million dollar gambling frenzy it generates, the Melbourne Cup is a high society extravaganza, a fashion parade at which the women display eccentric hats and a holiday during which rivers of beer and champagne flow and the whole country comes to a halt to watch the race and bet on the outcome. Founded in 1835, Melbourne is more elegant and aristocratic than any other Australian city. It developed in the mid-nineteenth century following the discovery of gold at Ballarat and Bendigo. The gold led to an explosion in its population, created a middle class and permitted the construction of magnificent homes and a network of public services. Thanks to its banks and the gold exchange, Melbourne became the financial capital of Australia, a position it held up to the 1960's and which it today shares with Sydney. On the declaration of independence in 1901, Melbourne became the provisional capital of the country while Canberra was being built. Today, with its three million, three hundred thousand inhabitants, it is Australia's second city and boasts the most prestigious university in the Antipodes organized along the lines of Oxford and Cambridge. The financial district is dominated by the Rialto, a mirror-plated tower, Australia's tallest office block topped by an observation deck on the fifty-fifth floor from which one can gaze out over the entire city. Melbourne is a multi-ethnic city with a wealth of faces, flavors and cultures from throughout the world. This can be seen in the crowds thronging the City, where the dark hair of the Mediterranean is mixed with the blonde manes of the Anglo-Saxons and the Oriental eyes of the Chinese. Nicknamed the Golden Mile, the City extends along the north bank of the Yarra River and is composed of a grid of around ten streets traversed by the same number of avenues. It is a triumph of architectural contrasts with Victorian Gothic Revival and neo-classical buildings reflected in the façades of glass-fronted tower blocks. The Melbourne that counts, however, lives to the south of the Yarra River, beyond the Royal Botanical Gardens, one of the world's most intriguing plant collections featuring lakes inhabited by black swans and surrounded by mature trees, lawns, flowerbeds and recreations of dry environments and jungles. The aristocracy can be found in Toorak Road, Australia's most elegant and exclusive residential address.

192-193 The state of Victoria contains a number of areas of temperate rain-forest, the remains of the damp jungle that once covered much of the eastern regions of the continent and which are today reduced to patches scattered along the mountainous backbone of the Great Dividing Range.

192 bottom The interior of the state of Victoria features the wild scenery of the Victoria Alps, mountains covered with forests and incised by torrents. These mountains are the backdrop to the legend of Ned Kelly, the bandit who was transformed into a national hero.

193 top This road in Victoria's Yarra Range National Park passes through a forest of towering eucalyptus trees. A native Australian tree, the eucalyptus is present in 600 species of the most diverse sizes, above all in the southern states of the continent. The highest examples are to be found in Tasmania and Western Australia.

193 bottom The Otway Promontory, to the south-west of Melbourne, boats one of the most spectacular areas of temperate rain-forest in Victoria. An area of imposing eucalyptus trees and enormous ferns amidst which fly various parrot species, such as the cacatua and the galah.

194 top The south coast of Tasmania is in part composed of cliffs. According to Aboriginal mythology, the stack dominating Cox Bight, a bay in the South West National Park, is an ancestor who after creating the island was launched into the air and fell back to earth, transforming himself into rock.

194-195 The landscape of Tasmania is scattered with large and small lakes overlooked by Alpine peaks. The area with the greatest number is known as the "Land of the Three Thousand Lakes" and is situated in the center of the island. The area stages international fishing matches.

Tasmania:

195 top *There are numerous livestock farms in Tasmania and one of the island's principal resources is its flock of 5 million Merino sheep that graze on the hillsides. They produce the wool with which the "Tasmania" cloth is woven, and exported throughout the world*

195 bottom *This photo shows the Alpine scenery of Cradle Mountain, a national park dominated by Mount Ossa, the highest peak in Tasmania (5,304 feet), featuring numerous waterfalls and crossed by the 50 miles of the Overland Track.*

an emerald green heart

Tasmania, an island the size of Ireland located to the south of Victoria, presents an image far removed from that typically associated with Australia. Here there are none of the boundless horizons, sun-baked deserts and blue skies of the continental mainland, but rather mountain ranges dotted with lakes, rugged moors and a damp climate tormented by frequent rains and the Roaring Forties, the winds of the lower latitudes. Situated between the 40th and 44th latitude south parallels, Tasmania has a complex coastline with dozens of smaller islands. It is separated from Victoria by the Bass Strait where King and Flinders Islands are to be found. The second of these was named after Matthew Flinders, the English captain who, in 1798, realized that Tasmania was itself an island. When the Dutch navigator, Abel Tasman, landed on its coasts for the first time in 1642, he had, in fact, presumed that he found himself on an extension of continental Australia, a land that in that era was almost completely unknown. Tasman baptized his discovery Van Diemens Land in honor of the governor of Batavia. It was renamed Tasmania in 1855 as a tribute to its discoverer. The island is traversed on the west side by a mountain range culminating in the 5,304-foot peak, Mount Ossa, in the Cradle Mountains region. This area features the 50-mile-long Overland Track, Australia's most renowned trekking route which attracts enthusiasts from all over the world. To the east of the Cradle Mountains is the Land of the Three Thousand Lakes, a watery mosaic at the very heart of the island. The Tasmanian landscape is made all the more unusual by the swathes of temperate rain forest that cover around a tenth of the territory and represent a third of all Australian damp climate environments and one of the last three such areas on the planet, together with those of New Zealand's South Island and northern Chile. The island's wildest scenery can be found in the South West National Park, an uninhabited area of around 1,737 square miles in which forests alternate with tundra and snow-covered peaks with fast-flowing streams and spectacular waterfalls. Together with the Franklin Lower Gordon National Park, the South West National forms a single great natural reserve. Through the former part runs the Franklin River, the tea-colored waters of which were at the center of one of the most famous ecological battles. The Tasmanian Wilderness Society, led by Bob Brown, opposed the construction of a dam with all the means at its disposal. Its militant members were imprisoned but the protest spread throughout Australia and forced the government to abandon the project. The environmental uniqueness of Tasmania also extends to its fauna. The island, which separated from the continent around 12,000 years ago, is home to two species of

carnivorous marsupials that have disappeared from the rest of Australia, the quoll, similar to a large squirrel, and the Tasmanian Devil, which is the size of a small dog and has needle-like teeth and black fur. *Thylacinus* or the Tasmanian Tiger, a 71-inch-long predatory marsupial with striped fur, is extinct, the last one dying in 1936. Thanks to this environmental sensitivity, over a fifth of the whole of Tasmania is protected as national parks and 11% of the territory has been inscribed in UNESCO's World Heritage List. When, in 1804, a group of English colonists settled at the mouth of the Derwent River, founding Hobart, the present-day capital of the state, Tasmania was inhabited by the most primitive and aggressive Aboriginal tribes of Australia. They lived completely naked, slept in bark bivouacs and were unable to reproduce fire. They ran through the forests carrying a kind of lantern they would use to regenerate their fires in one hand and a 10-foot hunting spear in the other. The impact of the white men was disastrous: following a series of battles with the colonist they sank into an inexorable decline. The last Tasmanian Aboriginal died in 1876. Today Tasmania is a prevalently an agricultural state, livestock farming being the mainstay of the economy with five million Merino sheep and half a million cattle grazing among the green hills of the north of the island. The other resources exploited by Tasmania's half a million inhabitants are tourism and mining, but it remains the most economically depressed of the Australian states with a high level of unemployment and a generally dated appearance. Hobart, with its low-rise buildings in the center and the fishing boats anchored in the port, could almost be a postcard scene from the Fifties.

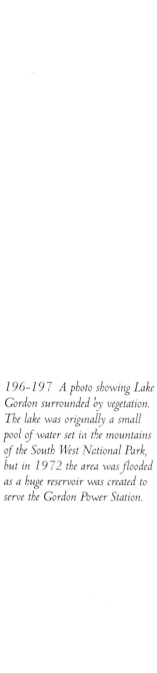

196-197 A photo showing Lake Gordon surrounded by vegetation. The lake was originally a small pool of water set in the mountains of the South West National Park, but in 1972 the area was flooded as a huge reservoir was created to serve the Gordon Power Station.

196 bottom Hobart is the small capital of Tasmania. Situated in the south coast of the island, it was founded in 1804 on the bay formed by the estuary of the Derwent River. Hobart was the second urban agglomeration in the history of Australia after Sydney.

197 top The Cradle Mountains National Park offers some of Tasmania's most spectacular scenery with steep summits reflected in large and small lakes. In spite of the relatively modest heights of its peaks (the highest stands at 5,304 feet) it is subject to storms in all seasons.

197 bottom Russell Falls are split on three levels amidst ferns and rocks shrouded with moss. They are the major attraction of the Mount Field National Park, a nature reserve with tree ferns, acacias and a variety of eucalyptus that grows to heights of up to 295 feet.

197

South Australia:

Were it not for Adelaide, where three-fifths of the population reside, this would be another frontier state. In South Australia, however, the desert, the Aboriginals and the rough outback lifestyle of the remote interior regions, coexist with the most British of the Australian capitals. This is the Australian state with the greatest percentage of desert land, yet the churches and golf courses surrounding the city of Adelaide appear to have been transposed from the English countryside. There are three distinct facets to South Australia: mining, agriculture and the coast. The exploitation of underground mineral resources takes on a picturesque and pioneering aspect in the subterranean city of Coober Pedy, the location of the world's greatest deposit of opals. An infernal place in the heart of the continent with temperatures exceeding 147° F, blasted by frequent dust storms and plagued by swarms of flies. In order to survive during their improbable quest for the seam of opals that will make them rich, the town's 4,000 inhabitants live in dugouts; that is, apartments equipped with stereo systems, air conditioning and even Jacuzzis, built into abandoned mine workings. No less remarkable is the lifestyle of the 4,000 inhabitants of the artificial city of Leigh Creek, built by the Electricity Trust of South Australia around a gigantic open-cast coal mine.

The grey-green mountains of the sinuous Flinders Ranges—a favored destination of walkers—separate Leigh Creek from the immense power stations of Playford near Port Augusta which it supplies with fuel. In spite of the looming presence of the mines, the state's greatest resource is actually agriculture. As bizarre as it might appear, given that much of the region is arid and uninhabited and the arable area is restricted to less than a tenth of the territory, the South Australians grow everything here, from cereals to vegetables, from citrus fruits to grapes. The Barossa Valley, located an hour's drive north from Adelaide, is in fact one of the principal Australian wine-making areas, its cellars containing an extraordinary variety of products from Lambrusco to Beaujolais, from Cabernet to Riesling. The majority of the wine producers are of German origins, their forebears migrating to South Australia in the mid-nineteenth century to escape the religious persecutions then afflicting Germany. From the somewhat Rhine-like climate of the Barossa Valley with its trellised houses and Weinstuben, to the Mediterranean atmosphere of Adelaide's Central Market where the Italian, Greek and Lebanese greengrocers display and proclaim the wonders of the local fruit and vegetables. The South Australian farmers live solitary lives on ranches in the vastness of the outback where they raise herds of cattle and immense flocks of sheep. Their contacts with civilization are guaranteed by the mail flights that each week depart from Port Augusta to supply them with fresh vegetables, news and chit-chat, while their children keep up with their schoolwork via lessons transmitted by radio. Despite having just a twelfth of the country's inhabitants—a million and a half individuals—South Australia contributes a third of the total national agricultural exports and 60% of the total wine production.

The state's coastal dependency is confirmed by the fact that the vast majority of its inhabitants live near the sea. The state boasts a wild coastline with miles of white sand locked between sandstone cliffs, such as those of Maslins Beach, the nudist beach half an hour's drive from the city. The sands of Kangaroo Island, one of the country's richest wildlife reserves, are inhabited by penguins and sea lions. Here in a single day you may observe kangaroos, koalas, opossums, emus, echidnae, anteaters and wombats as well as the Antarctic animals and 250 species of birds. Those who enjoy the sea most, however, are probably the

198-199 *The Flinders Ranges are composed of extremely ancient mountains dividing the fertile southern regions of South Australia from the desert plains and the salt lakes occupying much of the state.*

199 top *The Barossa valley is one of the best known Australian wine producing areas. Situated to the north of Adelaide, much of the valley is inhabited by the descendants of German immigrants who reached South Australia from Prussia and Silesia in 1842.*

wine, kangaroos, opals, corals e provincial life

200 top *The northern coast of Kangaroo Island, protected by Vincent Gulf, the bay on which Adelaide is situated, is the most suitable for bathing: the island boasts the long sands of Stokes Bay, Snelling Beach and above all, Emu Bay where the sea is rimmed by a white band stretching five miles.*

200 center *Fleurieu Peninsula extends to the south-east of Adelaide as far as Cape Jervis. The area boasts some of the most spectacular sands in South Australia including the nudist reserve of Maslins Beach, locked between sandstone cliffs, and Sellicks Beach (seen in this photo).*

inhabitants of Adelaide, a city in which a million people live along a 38-mile stretch of coastline, a fascinating succession of beaches. A quarter of the population lives just a few blocks from the ocean. Not that this makes a great difference, as this is a city designed with the car in mind and served by roads with three, four or even five lanes in each direction. They lead into the city, the rather run-down quarter revolving around King William Street, a commercial and service zone surrounded by a ring of parks with public sports facilities. Here there are no skyscrapers, traffic, crowds or night life. Founded in 1836 by the British colonists, Adelaide is quintessentially provincial and always lagging behind with respect to the technological innovations that continually redefine the other Australian capitals. A few somewhat questionable bars stay open until midnight in Hindley Street, the Mall—the pedestrian zone that appears to have been lifted wholesale from a German town—and is only ever crowded on a Thursday evening, the day on which the shops stay open for late-night shopping, and the Festival Center, an interesting example of modern architecture decorated with Aboriginal murals, only exploits its multi-media capabilities to the full every two years on the occasion of the Adelaide Arts Festival.

In spite of its muffled tones and rhythms, thanks to this arts extravaganza and the Bacchanal devoted to wine in the Barossa Valley, South Australia is described as the "Festival State."

200 bottom *One of the largest colonies (500 examples) of sea lions (Neophoca cinerea) in Australia lives on Seal Beach in Kangaroo Island's Cape Gantheaume Conservation Park. Cubs are born in the spring and are covered with a black fur that a few months later is replaced by a silver-grey pelt.*

201 *The immense Nullarbor Plain (the coastline of which is seen in the photo) divides the Adelaide region from the inhabited area of Western Australia, an infinite expanse of grey-green bushes traversed by an arrow-straight road running for 1,240 miles.*

Western Australia:

Western Australia accounts for a third of the entire surface area of the continent and best represents the image of the Australian frontier territory in which fortunes are still waiting to be made. Its enormous mineral deposits make it the richest state in Australia, and while it houses just a tenth of the Australian population it generates over a quarter of the gross national product. This was the first region of Australia to be discovered by the Europeans—the Dutchman Dirk Hartog landed here in 1616—but the last to be colonized. The British occupied it in 1829 only to frustrate French ambitions in the area. It only developed after 1890, once again following the discovery of gold deposits. Composed of a vast interior in which the desert dunes alternate with unusual rock formations, Western Australia also has a coastline stretching 7,765 miles which features rare islands and endless expanses white sand, such as Eighty Mile Beach to the south of Broome. To the north it is crowned by the continent's second largest coral reef, the Ningaloo Reef, a marine park covering 1,930 square miles that is home to 180 varieties of coral and 500 species of tropical fish. The most incredible site on the coast is, however, Monkey Mia, a bay where each day dolphins come into the shore, apparently in order to meet humans. The rangers provide fish for those visitors wishing to engage in close encounters with the animals, but frequently the

dolphins themselves approach the tourists with fish in their mouths in what the rangers believe is an attempt to communicate.

The red dunes of the Great Sandy Desert are traversed by herds of camels, introduced to Australia from Afghanistan in the late nineteenth centuries, complete with drivers in order to transport goods to the ranches of the outback. Following the construction of the railway, road and air networks, many animals were set loose in the wild where they found a favorable desert habitat and multiplied. Australia is now paradoxically the country with the world's largest camel population. In the Gibson Desert, instead, the last hunter-gatherers were found in 1984 a small group from the Pintubi tribe who had somehow escaped the meticulous combing of the continental interior during the Fifties when attempts were made to integrate the Aboriginals with white culture.

The greatest attractions of the interior of Western Australia are its rock formations. The wave-like West Rock is 50 feet high and its vertical stripes create an optical illusion of running water. The Pinnacles Desert is a sandy plain punctuated by thousands of calcareous spires up to 13 feet high, while in the northern region of the Kimberley there is the timeless landscape of the Bungle Bungles, an area covering 3,000 square miles covered with thousands of cones of sandstone up to 656 feet high. Orange rocks alternate with black strata composed of fossilized algae and deep gorges in which an endemic species of palm tree grows. The Kimberley also boasts the world's largest diamond mine, at Lake Argyle, extracting 34 million carats a year. The majority of the stones are impure diamonds used for industrial purposes, but among the few high quality gems found here are there extremely rare pink diamonds. These are the most precious treasures of a state whose underground resources include rich deposits of uranium, gold, bauxite, iron, zinc, nickel, lead, copper, coal, oil and natural gas. Mining has supported the economy of Western Australia even during the periods when the rest of the country was depressed. Perth, the state capital, has never lost its appeal for immigrants: it was the only Australian city not to have suffered from the recession of the late Eighties and to have reacted positively to the Asian crisis of the late Nineties.

Isolated from the rest of the country, Perth is the Australian city where one experiences the "tyranny of

202-203 The extravagant rock formations of the Pinnacles Desert are found in the south coast of Western Australia. The pinnacles, calcareous columns varying from a few inches to 13 feet in height are scattered across a broad, flat sandy plain.

203 top Ayers Rock is the monolith rising at the very center of Australia. A rocky dome with a circumference of 5.5 miles, it changes color during the day from brown through pink, orange, red, violet, blue and black as the sun moves across the sky.

sailing boat, diamonds and infinite deserts

distance" most acutely. Adelaide, its nearest city neighbor, is three days' drive away, while reaching Sydney involves a five-hour flight. With respects to the East coast, Perth might just as well be on a different continent. Founded in 1829 as the British outpost on the banks of the river Swan, it developed into a city following the 1890 Gold Rush. Today it is a metropolis with futuristic highways directing streams of cars towards the skyscrapers of the City, a concrete and glass commercial district surrounded by a green lung of parkland extending over 380 square miles. Endless residential districts of detached houses set in gardens stretch along the coasts to the north and south of the city center. Perth forms a single great urban conglomeration with Fremantle, the major Australian Indian Ocean port, and accommodates 1,400,000 inhabitants. Fremantle is particularly famous among sailing enthusiasts as it is a customary port of call for the Whitbread Round the World Race, and a boat built here, the *Australia II*, won the America's Cup in 1983. Apart from sailing, Fremantle is characterized by its cultural life with theaters, art galleries and music pubs. Infinite white sand beaches link Fremantle with central Perth, along with the metropolitan railway and the ferries that shuttle across the waters of the estuary.

205 center Perth (seen from King's Park in this photo) is the capital of Western Australia. It was founded in 1829 on the banks of the River Swan. Isolated from the rest of the country, over the last decade it has been the most dynamic city with the highest rate of growth in Australia.

205 bottom The Bungle Bungle rock formations are to be found in the Kimberley region. A timeless landscape covering an area of 3,000 square miles, with hundreds of 656-foot-high cones formed of strata of sandstone alternating with strata of sedimented black algae.

204 The Ningaloo Reef is a coral structure situated off the north coast of Western Australia. It is composed of 180 species of coral and was formed 15 million years ago. The reef encloses a lagoon in which swim 500 species of fish.

205 top Perth, and above all its port suburb of Fremantle, boast a number of pubs dating back to the colonial era. Large buildings surrounded by porticoes and magnificent verandas with fine fretwork decoration in wood. As well as serving beer they offer live music.

206-207 The Kalbarri National Park (Western Australia) is crossed by the River Murchison which before flowing into the Indian Ocean traces some wonderful scenery. In the southern hemisphere winter cf July and August, the park is ablaze with the flowering of many wild plants.

206 bottom Chamberlain Gorge (seen here in this photo) is one of the many canyons encountered in the wild Kimberley region in the extreme north-east of Western Australia. Among the most spectacular in the area are Barnett River Gorge and Emma Gorge.

207 top An aerial photo showing the Haeding dam in Pilbara, the northern region producing most of Western Australia's mineral wealth. This is an inhospitable land with torrid summers alternating with cold, wet winters. The situation is made all the worse by the hurricanes which regularly blast the mining villages.

207 bottom Situated close to Broome, the largest town in the north of Western Australia, Gantheaume Point features the most significant remains of the Jurassic Period to have been found on the continent: gigantic dinosaur footprints which according to the palaeontologists are 130 million years old.

The Northern Territory represents the final frontier of a world of pioneers. Partially uninhabited (it boasts a population density of just a single human being every 3 square miles), as its name suggests it is a territory rather than a state and so the federal government has the right to intervene in its internal affairs. This could hardly be otherwise in such a vast area occupying over a sixth of the country as a whole whilst accommodating less than one percent of its inhabitants. Among the rocks of the Red Center and the swamps of the Kakadu National Park, the Northern Territory contains some of Australia's most intriguing landscapes and many of its national myths. In pride of place there is Ayers Rock, the world's largest monolith. A block of sandstone that was formed through the process of sedimentation 600 million years ago, the very heart of Australia and surely its most famous postcard scene. It is, however, also a sacred site for many Aboriginal tribes living in the central regions to whom it is known as Uluru—Mother Earth—and who celebrate ancestral rituals and initiation ceremonies in the caverns opening onto its slopes. Standing in front of Ayers Rock is Mount Olgas, a cluster of 36 rock domes that, like the

have over the ages eroded 13 gorges that in a 7.5-mile-long geological chain alternate with violent rapids. This drama contrasts with the arid flatness of Never Never Land, the infinite plain bordering Queensland, across which the vast herds typical of the north-eastern regions roam. The Northern Territory's most sensational landscape can, however, be found in the Kakadu National Park, the vast swamp inhabited by gigantic salt-water crocodiles where the film *Crocodile Dundee* was filmed. The 6,540 square miles of this immense region extend from the coast of the Arafura Sea to a sandstone buttress supporting a huge rocky plateau. Over more than a billion years this landscape has been modelled by drastic climatic changes that alternated floods with fires. A mosaic of rivers, damp forests, marshes, waterfalls and rocks which contains some of the oldest and most important archaeological sites in Australia. Carbon 14 testing has dated the graffiti of Obiri Rock to 23,000 years ago and historians have estimated that the Gagadju Aboriginals were present in the region 40,000 years ago. The park is the most extraordinary wildlife reserve anywhere in Australia with almost 500 species of birds, mammals, reptiles, amphibians and fish being cataloged along with 10,000 insects. These factors have led to Kakadu's inclusion in UNESCO's World Heritage List.

Each state has the capital it deserves and the Northern Territory sees itself reflected in Darwin, the hottest, wildest and most exotic city in Australia. Founded in 1869 as a port for gold-miners, it later developed as a telegraph station. Its center is composed of a few grid-pattern streets lined with modern buildings that were rebuilt after Cyclone Tracy struck in 1974. It is more of a frontier post between Australia and Asia than a city. The Oriental community is so numerous that in the late Eighties it managed to elect a Chinese mayor, and the Chinese are the

Northern Territory: the deserts and swamps of Crocodile Dundee

major formation, change color throughout the day according to the position of the sun. Other spectacular rock formations can be found around Alice Springs, the town in the center of the continent that was founded in 1870 as a telegraph station linking the south of the country and Darwin. In the MacDonnell Range, which splits central Australia from east to west, there are around ten canyons but also imposing monoliths such as Chambers Pillar and the dozen gigantic craters—caused by falling meteorites—composing the lunar landscape of Henbury. The Northern Territory is the region of Australia with the strongest Aboriginal influence. Almost a quarter of the population belongs to around fifty tribes to which more land has been returned than in any other region of the country. The territory houses immense Aboriginal reserves such as Arnhem Land in the Top End and Tiwi on Melville Island. Alice Springs is the most important center of modern Aboriginal art. Thousands of rock paintings and engravings are scattered throughout the area and the annual tribal festivals of Yendumu and Barunga attract thousands of Aboriginals to exhibitions of painting and sculpture combined with sporting events. Barunga is located near Katherine, a one-street town—like many in the outback—that owes its existence to the appeal of one of the continent's most spectacular canyons: on a plateau of red calcareous rock, the waters of the Katherine River

strongest ethnic group among the sixty that make-up the city's racial kaleidoscope. The Chinese inhabitants live alongside the last of the hippies who commute between Darwin—generous dispenser of reasonably-paid non-skilled jobs—and the nearby East. Then there are the tourists who, in search of a picturesque last frontier, entrust themselves to the bushmen with their wide-brimmed Akubra hats, sun-burned faces and tattoos, who accompany them on excursions into the Kakadu National Park. At Darwin, as throughout the Northern Territory, all the white people appear to be merely passing through: the city has an official population of 80,000, but there is a remarkable turnover and the city is an incredible crucible of diverse destinies.

210-211 The whale shark (Rhiniodon typus) is the largest of the 350 species of shark found in Oceania. This underwater photograph was taken off the Ningaloo Reef, Australia's second largest barrier reef situated off the north-west coast.

210 bottom A whitetip reef shark (Triaenodon obesus) swimming in the company of a remora. This predator lives in coastal waters with sandy sea beds where it swims between the surface and depths of up to 1,080 feet. The shark is over 6.5 feet long and feeds on bottom dwelling fish.

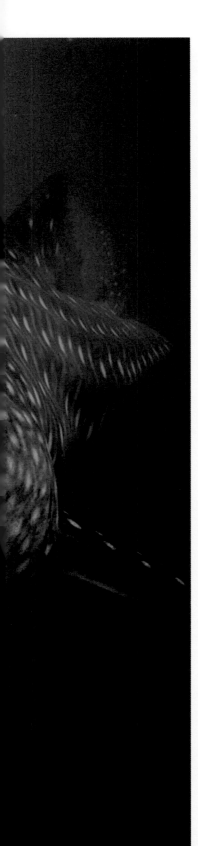

WONDERS OF THE PACIFIC OCEAN FLOOR

The majority of the organisms that live in the blue immensity of the Pacific Ocean originated at the margins of the vastest of the oceans. Marine biologists have, in fact, come to the conclusion that the fauna of the Indian and Pacific Oceans had a single source, the triangle of sea (which according to the geographic conventions belongs to the Indian Ocean) between the Philippines, New Guinea, the northern coast of Australia and the Malay Peninsula. In this region where the world's greatest density of islands is to be found (the archipelagos of Indonesia and the Philippines contain over twenty thousand), the evolution of myriad marine species has been possible thanks to a great variety of habitats and to ecosystems that have remained fundamentally stable through many geological eras. Even though the evolution of its fauna took place beyond its borders, the Pacific contains the most extraordinary, variegated and numerous forms of marine life. From the most microscopic forms of phytoplankton to gigantic whales, from the thousands of species of brilliantly colored tropical fish to the frightening salt-water crocodiles, from the thousands of species of molluscs to the vast shoals of tuna, from the deadly but virtually invisible jellyfish to the great colonies of sea lions, from the six species of sea turtles to the sharks of almost all the species recorded anywhere on the planet. Then there are the most extraordinary examples of biological architecture, the coral reefs. If the abysses of the Pacific (the ocean has an average depth of 13,100 feet with the world's deepest point at 36,152 feet being recorded in the Mariana Trench in Micronesia) are the last frontier of oceanographic research, the coral reefs are the most intensively studied and complex of marine ecosystems. The Pacific contains the Great Barrier Reef, the largest in the world, a coral fringe extending for 1,240 miles and covering an area equivalent to that of Great Britain, situated off the north-east coast of Australia, between the Tropic of Capricorn and New Guinea. New Caledonia instead features the planet's second longest reef at 994 miles. According to the oceanographer Jacques-Yves Cousteau, the best Pacific waters for diving and the observation of fauna are, however, to be found off Fiji's small Rainbow Reef, 19 miles of coral linking the islands of Vanua Levu and Taveuni. The Fijian islands also boast the record for submarine visibility with the naked eye able to see 246 feet off the Astrolabe Reef, the 25-mile ring encircling the island of Kadavu. The visibility in the internal lagoons of the atolls, particularly Rangiroa in the Tuamotu archipelago, is also remarkable, albeit officially restricted to 82-98 feet in depth.

The waters at the center of the atolls of Micronesia and the Northern Group of the Cook Islands, as well in the Tuamotu archipelago, are responsible for the most intense colors in the Pacific, almost surreal blues in which the fluorescent scales of many of the lagoon fish traces fantastic chromatic contrasts.

The coral reefs were formed between two and eighteen million years ago as a result of the actions of coral polyps, molluscs just a couple of inches long encased in calcareous skeletons which grow together, adhere and eventually form coralline rocks. This process gradually raises the reef until it reaches the surface of the water. The biological complexity of these ecosystems

derives from the over 600 species of coral (including dozens of soft species with no calcareous skeletons), thousands of species of pelagic fish and crustaceans and tens of thousands of invertebrates. Bizarre animals such as the dugong (Dugong dugon) or sea cow, a large marine mammal that may reach up to ten feet in length and 1,323 pounds in weight, can be found among the corals. The dugong belongs to the Sirenian order, has bilobate caudal flippers, a rounded head and prominent pectoral mammary glands. The female gives birth in the water. Hunted for centuries for their meat and oil, the dugong is today protected because it is considered to be an endangered species. Around 10,000 examples survive in the Pacific where its greatest enemies are sharks.

In the northern waters of the Great Barrier Reef, off New Guinea, the sharks engage in titanic duels with the most ferocious inhabitants of the ocean, the salt-water crocodiles (Crocodylus porosus). These giants grow to up to 23 feet in length and in the water attack their prey at a

speed of 28 miles per hour. Extraordinary swimmers, salt-water crocodiles undertake extremely long migrations from the Bay of Bengal (India) to the Melanesian archipelagos by way of the Arafura Sea and the Coral Sea. 350 of the 370 shark species present in the oceans can be found in the waters of Oceania. They include the flying, hammerhead, cigar, saw, elephant, leopard, cat, angel, bullhead and fox sharks as well as the largest of all, the whale shark. Twenty-eight species are known to have attacked man, with the most aggressive being the tiger, bull and white sharks, this last growing up to 23 feet in length. The danger posed by sharks has, however, been blown out of all proportion. Taking into consideration the hundreds of millions of bathers, you are more likely to win a major lottery than to be eaten by a shark who has more to fear from man than vice versa.

The tiger and hammerhead sharks are considered to be endangered species, while each year a hundred million

sharks are caught to supply the fish markets of Australia, the United States, Japan and China where the flavorsome white meat is served with a variety of sauces.

Meanwhile, the hunting of the ocean's largest inhabitants has virtually ceased and the majority of the world's eighty species of whales can be found in the Pacific. They generally live in the Polar regions, but many species reproduce in the warm waters of the tropics which they reach after awe-inspiring migratory journeys. The grey whales, for example leave the freezing waters of the Bering Sea each year heading for the lagoons of Baja California (Mexico). Around 6,000 examples (of the 18,000 estimated to inhabit the Pacific) form a caravan that, at a cruising speed of six miles per hour, cover a distance of almost five thousand miles. Whales can be seen in most of the Pacific, from Hawaii to New Zealand, from Australia to Fiji. Their enormous arching backs, topped by the classic spouts generated by exhaled air and foam, are most easily seen in fine weather, heavy seas making them much more difficult to spot. The most spectacular encounters are those with the sperm whales (Physeter macrocephalus) which can be seen off Kaikoura in New Zealand where, between October and August, numerous whale watchers arrive by sea and by air. The sperm whale is the largest of the odontocetes with the males reaching up to 62 feet in length and weighing up to seventy tons. They are distinguished from other whales by their great rectangular heads The waters of New Zealand are also inhabited by the pilot whale (Globicephala melaena) and the Hector's dolphin (Cephalorhynchus hectori), this last being the smallest of the sixty-two dolphin species recorded in Oceania. At Monkey Mia on the south-west coast of Australia dolphins are the protagonists in one of the most intriguing examples of communication with man. Every day during the winter and frequently during the summer too, dozens of examples arrive in Shark Bay at regular times with the sole apparent aim of meeting human beings. The dolphin family also includes the so-called killer whale (Orcinus orca), a 30-foot-long cetacean with a voracious appetite for seals and fish. Marine legends have grown up around the presumed aggressiveness of the killer whale, but in reality attacks on man have never been documented. Apart from the dolphins which can be seen in many areas, the most common cetacean in the Southern Seas is the hunchback whale (Megaptera novaengliae). Each year thousands of examples migrate from Antarctica, passing by way of New Zealand to the warm waters of Fiji and the Great Barrier Reef to celebrate their mating season.

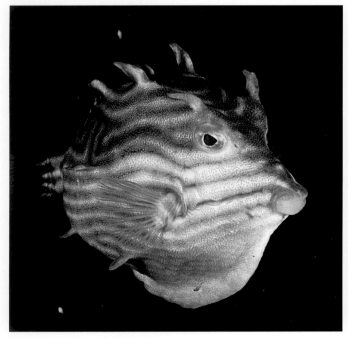

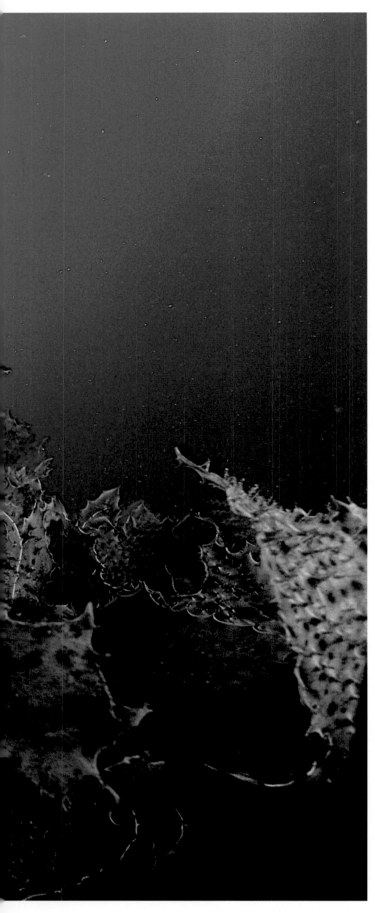

216-217 The Sea Dragon (Phyllopterix taeniolatus) is one of the most bizarre animals recorded in the tropical waters of northern Australia. The long nose and the shape of the mouth are the weapons it uses to capture its prey

216 bottom left This underwater photo shows the cowfish, a symbol of the Governor Island Marine Park off Bicheno in Tasmania (Southern Australia): similar to a tropical boxfish, the cowfish is a typical inhabitant of the cold seas of the lower latitudes.

216 bottom right The Australian giant cuttlefish may reach up to three feet in length. The photographer could hardly believe his eyes when, during the exploration of the waters of Jervis Bay in New South Wales, he spotted this authentic marine monster.

217 top In the waters off Tasmania (the large island to the south of Australia) banks of coral, for the most part sea fans and whips and candelabra-like sponges of the most remarkable colors can be found amidst forests of kelp.

217 center The large candelabra-like orange sponges are the best known features of the waters off Bicheno (Tasmania) where, in the month of August, in the middle of the southern hemisphere's winter, the sea can be so clear as to allow excellent underwater vision.

217 bottom In the waters of Jervis Bay in New South Wales (south-east Australia) one may encounter brightly colored forms of life such as sea-horses, pink and yellow sponges and starfish with the diameter of a football amidst the algae and kelp forests.

218 top *The yellowish, gas-filled vesicles at the base of each strand of kelp. These small tanks help to keep the plant extended vertically to that it can reach the surface of the water and receive sunlight.*

218 center *A diver cautiously approaches a sand-tiger shark (Eugomphodus taurus), easily recognizable thanks to its unusual jaws with long pointed teeth at the front and molar-like teeth at the back. This predator lives close to the bottom in coastal waters with depths of 650 feet or over.*

218 bottom *The Port Jackson shark (Heterodontus portusjacksoni) is a member of the heterodont order with a cylindrical body tapering towards the rear and wider at the front due to the conical head. The species lives above all along the coatss of Australia and New Zealand at depths ranging from the surface to over 550 feet.*

218-219 *A diver uses his torch to illuminate the long ramifications of a kelp forest. The giant variety of this submarine plant may exceed 65 feet in length and grows at an extraordinary speed. Anchored to the rocks of the sea bed, this algae reaches the surface of the water in order to be able to capture the rays of the sun and activate the process of photosynthesis essential for its survival. This photo was taken in the underwater paradise of the Tasman Sea.*

219 bottom This spectacular photo taken in the waters off Tasmania shows a group of playful sea lions fascinated by the photographer's lens. These mammals are one of the favorite targets of the great predators, above all the white shark.

220-221 At Cod Hole, at the heart of the Great Barrier Reef, giant groupers (Epinephelus tauvina) tolerate encounters with the divers that manage to approach their lairs as long as they are not carrying any food. These members of the Serranidae family are in spite of their bulk, sociable and have on numerous occasions demonstrated that they have no fear of man.

220 bottom left This photo was taken in the waters of the Fijian archipelago where Rainbow Reef is to be found, according to the oceanographer Jacques-Yves Cousteau, one of the best areas of the Pacific Ocean for diving and the observation of fauna.

220 bottom right An underwater photo taken in the waters of New South Wales. As can be seen, a dense shoal of silvery fish is opening to allow the passage of a diver.

221 top The Pacific Ocean is a veritable paradise for divers who can explore almost all the Polynesian, Micronesian and Melanesian archipelagos as well as the remarkable waters of Australia's Great Barrier Reef. In this photo, the brilliant colors of the soft corals, around which pulses the extraordinary life of the reef, have captured the attention of the photographer.

221 bottom This group of silvery jacks (Caranx sexfasciatus) was photographed in the lagoon of Flinders Reed, one of the banks of coral composing the Australian Great Barrier Reef. These fish swim in such dense formations that a kind of wall is formed that reflects a metallic gleam from torches or flashes that illuminates the blue depths of the ocean.

222 top *These gigantic* Alcyonacea *are typical of the Coral Sea. It is in fact rare to see examples of this size elsewhere in the Pacific. This species, yellow in the photo, can be found in a vast range of colors.*

222 center *A diver exploring the waters of the Australian Great Barrier Reef with (on the left) a large sea-fan which is exposed to the flow of the current so as to capture the micro-organisms that aid its nutrition.*

222-223 *The branching of this sea-fan is so delicate as to allow the shape of a diver to be seen behind it. This is a variety of coral belonging to the Gorgonacea order and principally develops in bushy and tree-like colonies that grow across the currents to as to capture the microorganisms on which they feed.*

223 bottom left *The soft* Alcyonacea *of the Australian Great Barrier reef grow to incredible dimensions. The high density of these soft coral trees has led to an area of the Coral Sea being nicknamed the Softwood Forest.*

223 bottom right *Divers in the waters of the Coral Sea will encounter the sensational spectacle of brilliantly colored, gigantic sea-fans. Large yellow sea-fans also grow within submarine channels.*

222 bottom *Soft corals of the* Alcyonacea *order grow to stunning sizes within the Flinders Reef lagoon (Great Barrier Reef). Such is their bulk that at times they are reminiscent of the baobabs found in the bush of Western Australia.*

224 Sunset at Tahiti with the volcanic peaks of Moorea rising beyond the palms. Both islands belong, together with Tetiaroa, Maiao and Mehetia, to the Windward Islands group of the Society Islands.

Archivio White Star: pages 16-17, 18-19, 22 bottom, 26, 27 bottom, 28, 29, 30, 31, 32 bottom, 33 top and bottom, 34 bottom, 34-35, 35 bottom, 36, 36-37, 37, 42 bottom. **Antonio Attini / Archivio White Star:** pages 50 top, 84, 85, 86-87, 86 bottom, 87 top and bottom, 90 left top and bottom, 90 right top and bottom. **Marcello Bertinetti / Archivio White Star:** pages 1, 52 bottom, 57 center, 56 center, 56 right, 57 bottom, 81 top and bottom, 78 and 79 bottom, 82 left top, 82 right top, 82 left bottom and right bottom, 83, 224. **Giulio Veggi / Archivio White Star:** pages 158 bottom, 167 top, 182 left bottom and right center, 183 top, 186, 187, 188 top, 189, 205 center. **AKG Photo:** pages 17 top, 25 top and bottom, 34 top, 41, 44 top, 44-45. **Kelvin Aitken / Panda Photo:** pages 107, 108-109, 109 top, 135 top, 136 top, 150-151, 214 top. **Giulio Andreini:** pages 118 bottom, 123 top, 128 top, 128-129, 129 bottom, 130 top, 131, 132 bottom, 133. **Philippe Bacchet:** page 14-15. **Franco Banfi:** page 110-111. **Gary Bell / Planet Earth Pictures:** page 6-7. **Michel Bennetts / Hedgehog House:** page 70 center right. **Carlo Borlenghi / Sea & See:** page 67 bottom. **Kathy Cashman / Hedgehog House:** page48-49. **Peter Chadwick / ABPL Image Library:** page195 bottom. **Graham Charles / Hedgehog House:** page 71. **Stefano Cellai:** pages 54 bottom, 62-63. **COO-EE Historical Picture Library:** page16 bottom. **G. Costa / Ag. Stradella:** pages 19 top, 24 top. **Matthieu Colin / Hémisphères:** page157. **Guido Cozzi / Atlantide:** pages 6 top, 87 center, 92-93, 92 top, 94 bottom, 95, 178 top, 198 top, 200 center. **G. Cubitt / Panda Photo:** pages 127 right top and bottom. **C. Dani - I. Jeske / Ag. Franca Speranza:** page173 bottom. **Digital Vision:** page 159 top. **E.T. Archive:** pages 18 bottom, 24-25, 44 bottom. **Mary Evans Picture Library:** pages 39 top, 45 top. **Jean-Paul Ferrero / Ardea London Ltd.:** pages 9, 94-95, 109. **Stanislas Fautre / Ask Images / Ag. Franca Speranza:** page61 top. **Fototeca Storica Nazionale:** pages 17 bottom, 22 top, 40 top. **Stéphane Frances / Hémisphères:** page118-119. **Bertrand Gardel / Hémisphères:** pages 60-61, 60 bottom, 169 bottom. **Geo Image Library:** page 180. **Martin Harvey / ABPL Image Library:** page173 top. **Martin Harvey / Panda Photo:** page8 bottom. **Johanna Huber / SIME:** pages 8 center, 166 top, 178-179, 196-197, 196 bottom, 206-207. **Klein Hubert / Panda Photo:** page 126, 193 bottom. **H. Hughes / Visa Agence photographique:** page 58-59. **J. M. La Roque / Ardea London Ltd.:** page 188-189. **Library of Congress:** page 21 bottom. **Maurizio Leigheb:** pages 13, 119 bottom, 124, 125, 134-135, 136-137, 137 bottom, 140, 141, 142-143, 144, 145, 146-147, 149 top. **Mitchell Library / State Library of New South Australia:** page 38 bottom. **Ugo Monetti:** pages 47 center, 50 bottom, 52 top and 53 top, 55 top, 57 top, 56 bottom, 80 bottom, 81 center, 72 top, 73 top and center, 76 bottom, 77, 88, 89 bottom, 90 left center, 106 bottom, 109 bottom, 110 bottom left, 111, 116, 117, 118 top, 123 bottom, 152, 153, 154, 155, 156 center left and center right, 159 bottom, 170, 171 center left, and center right, 178 center, 202 top, 203 top, 205 top and center, 208 top. **Marco Moretti:** pages 2-3, 12-13, 12 bottom, 51 top, 54 top, 56 left, 64 top, 74 top and bottom, 75, 96, 97, 99 top, 100-101, 101, 104 bottom, 104-105, 105 bottom, 129 top, 130 center and bottom, 132-133, 184 bottom, 185 top. **Colin Monteath / Hedgehog House:** page 127 left bottom. **Colin Monteath / Mountain Camera:** page 68-69, 68 bottom. **National Library of Australia, Canberra / The Bridgeman Art Library:** pages 24 bottom, 38-39. **The National Maritime Museum, Greenwich:** pages 26-27, 32-33. **Aldo Pavan:** pages 64 bottom, 65 bottom, 166-167, 168 top. **Doug Perrine / Innerspace Visions:** pages 48 bottom, 76 center, 99 bottom, 122-123, 148-149, 148 top and bottom. **Photobank:** pages 4-5, 49 top, 61 bottom, 72-73, 98-99, 98 bottom, 102-103, 102 bottom, 110 bottom right, 122 top, 134 top and bottom, 136 bottom, 138-139, 150 top, 151 top and bottom, 158-159, 177, 181, 182, 197 top, 198-199, 198 bottom, 199 top, 202 bottom, 202-203. **Photo Index / Panda Photo:** page 171 bottom. **John Noble / Wilderness Photographic Library:** page 197 bottom. **Andrea Pistolesi:** page 63 bottom, 64-65, 66-67, 66 bottom right, 67 top, 70 top, 70 center left, 70 bottom, 75 bottom, 78-79, 167 bottom, 200 top and bottom, 205 bottom, 206 bottom. **Fabrizia Postiglione / Focus Team:** pages 174-175, 176-177, 193 top. **Private Collection / The Bridgeman Art Library:** pages 40-41, 42-43, 45 bottom. **N. Renaudeau / Hoa-Qui / Ag. Franca Speranza:** page 80-81. **Roberto Rinaldi:** pages 6 bottom, 57, 78-79, 82-83, 112, 113, 114, 115, 156 top and bottom, 172-173, 172 top, 183 bottom right, 184-185, 185 bottom, 194-195, 194 top, 195 top, 210 bottom, 211, 214 bottom, 215 bottom, 216, 217, 218, 219, 220, 221, 222, 223. **René Robert / Agence Freestyle:** page69 bottom. **Jeff Rotman:** pages 106 center, 108 top, 208 bottom, 210-211, 212-213. **Royal Geographical Society:** page39 bottom, **P. Ryan / Panda Photo:** page 171 top. **Giovanni Simeone / SIME:** page 88-89. **Jess Stock - Stock Shot:** page 69 top. **The British Library / The Bridgeman Art Library:** page 20. **Ph. Tauqueur / Ag. Franca Speranza:** page 168-169. **Angelo Tondini / Focus Team:** page 52-53. **Nico Tondini / Ag. Focus Team:** pages 12 top, 54-55, 63 top, 93 top, 93 bottom, 100 bottom, 102 top, 103 bottom, 104 top, 176 top, 178 bottom. **Yvan Travert / Ag. Franca Speranza:** page190-191. **Trevern & Anna Dawes / Ag. Franca Speranza:** page 168 bottom. **Clerie Vasas / Kelvin Aitken Photography:** page 204. **J. D. Watt / Innerspace Visions:** page 91. **J. D. Watt / Panda Photo:** page 214.